WELLESLEY
1846-1937

WITH STRANGE SURPRISE

by
WALTER FANCUTT

The Leprosy Mission
50 Portland Place
London, W1N 3DG

Copyright © 1974 by *The Leprosy Mission*.
First printed in Great Britain 1974.
reprinted 1977
ISBN 0 902731 13 0.

All rights reserved. No part of this publication may be reproduced or transmitted in any form or by any means, electronic or mechanical, including photocopy, recording, or any information storage or retrieval system, without permission in writing from the publisher. This book is sold subject to the condition that it shall not, by way of trade or otherwise, be lent, re-sold, hired out or otherwise circulated without the publisher's prior consent in any form of binding or cover other than that in which this is published and without a similar condition including this condition being imposed on the subsequent purchaser.

Printed in Great Britain for
The Leprosy Mission, 50 Portland Place, London W1N 3DG
by David Green (Printers) Ltd., Kettering, Northants.

DEDICATION

To the pioneers of the past in grateful memory; to my colleagues of today, in sincere admiration; to those who will follow, that they may complete the task which Wellesley Bailey began.

CONTENTS

	Introduction	9
Chapter I	EARLY LIFE	11
Chapter II	PIONEERS! O PIONEERS	15
Chapter III	A NEW BEGINNING	21
Chapter IV	A MISSION IS BORN	28
Chapter V	HOW FAR CAN WE GO?	33
Chapter VI	IN STEP WITH THE MASTER	40
Chapter VII	IN JOURNEYINGS OFT	46
Chapter VIII	THE HERO OF MOLOKAI	51
Chapter IX	THE ROAD TO CHANDAG	55
Chapter X	OPEN DOORS IN THE FAR EAST	58
Chapter XI	THE FIRST NATIONAL AUXILIARY	62
Chapter XII	COLLEAGUES AT HOME	65
Chapter XIII	TOURS AND CONFERENCES	69
Chapter XIV	"RECEIVE INTO YOUR CUSTODY"	75
Chapter XV	BEYOND THE SKY-LINE	79
Chapter XVI	THE THICK CLOUD	88
Chapter XVII	THE CLOSING YEARS	94
Chapter XVIII	THROUGH GATES OF SPLENDOUR	102

INTRODUCTION

During the early years of the 1870's three men who were unknown to each other found themselves facing the same problem, though living and working in widely separated areas of the world.

The first was a Norwegian doctor, working in Bergen; the second a Belgian priest, working in Honolulu; and the third an Irish schoolmaster, working in India.

Differing tremendously in background, training and religion, they shared a common concern—LEPROSY.

The doctor was Gerard Armauer Hansen who discovered and studied the bacillus which caused the disease and did much to bring men's thoughts towards the proper understanding of a disease which, all too often, had been treated as a stigma and a curse. His initial discovery of the leprosy bacillus was made on February 28th, 1873, and he gave the rest of his life to leprosy research.

The priest was Father Damien de Veuster who sailed for Honolulu as a Missionary, and heard, in May 1873, of the plight of Hawaiian leprosy sufferers who were forced to live in exile on the Island of Molokai. He pleaded with his Bishop for the opportunity to serve the unfortunate sufferers, even though he knew it would mean voluntary exile on his own part. Within a few hours of his request being granted, Father Damien was sailing for Molokai, where he served the leprosy sufferers until he himself contracted the disease and died in 1889.

The schoolmaster was Wellesley C. Bailey who, at the time Doctor Hansen was pursuing his studies in Bergen, and Father Damien was sailing for Molokai, had already been helping to meet the needs of leprosy sufferers in North India for four years and was preparing to return to Ireland because of his wife's health. But, unknown to him, the seeds of his life's work were already germinating and he was to give more than forty years of service to the victims of leprosy. It is the story of this one man's fight for leprosy sufferers that we shall tell in the chapters which follow. Wellesley Bailey neither sought nor shunned the great responsibilities which faced him in his discipleship. He found his vocation, in Francis Thompson's phrase, "with strange surprise", believing:

> *Some may perchance with strange surprise*
> *Have blundered into paradise.*
> *In vasty dusk of life abroad,*
> *They fondly thought to err from God,*
> *Nor knew the circle that they trod;*
> *And, wandering all the night about,*
> *Found them at dawn where they set out.*
> *Death dawned; heaven lay in prospect wide—*
> *Lo! they were standing by His side!*

Chapter I

EARLY LIFE

My heart leaps up when I behold
A rainbow in the sky:
So was it when my life began;
So is it now I am a man
So be it when I shall grow old,
Or let me die!
The Child is Father of the Man;
And I could wish my days to be
Bound each to each by natural piety.
                              William Wordsworth

The Ireland into which Wellesley Bailey was born in 1846, was still suffering from the aftermath of the Napoleonic wars which had left a legacy of poverty and social unrest. The famine years from 1817 to 1822 were but the tragic precursors of the still greater potato famines which decimated Ireland in the 1840s.

More than a million people died within five years, with starvation and cholera as the main causes, while hundreds of thousands fled to England and America, or emigrated to the new colonies of the Queen.

Wellesley Bailey's father was the Agent for the Cosby Stradballey Estate (hence Wellesley's second name) and the family home Thornberry, near Abbeyleix in Queen's County, was a spacious country house, standing in its own grounds as a symbol of the Augustan age of Queen Anne.

The family was prosperous enough to send Wellesley

and his three brothers to Kilkenny College, a boarding academy which seems to have had its share of near famine conditions, for Wellesley remembered, many years later, the college suppers which consisted of bread and water seasoned with pepper and salt to disguise their inadequacy.

There was a good deal of banter and ragging at the college but the four boys were able to stand together as a group. More vulnerable were two brothers named Swift who came in for a lot of persecution from the other boys because their father showed an interest in the possibility of air travel—considered a dangerous, even disgraceful and irreligious investigation in those days.

When the boys were home from college, they joined their sisters in attending Stradbally church where they had been baptized and, indirectly, one such visit was to have a tremendous influence upon Wellesley's life. The young Baileys arrived at the church so late that they dared not go down the aisle to the family pew. Instead they crept upstairs to the gallery, only to find another family of youngsters—the Grahames—in the same predicament. The two groups decided to join forces for a day's outing. With a picnic lunch and fishing rods, all seemed set for a happy time, but the boys of the two families quarrelled and came to blows, while the girls tried to bring peace and decorum. One of the girls, Alice Mary Grahame, must have created a good impression on Wellesley for she later became his wife! Not that she was the only star in his young sky in those early days. There was an occasion when Wellesley was returning to Kilkenny College and Alice brought him a rosebud, while her rival brought him a purse. He solved the problem and salved his conscience, by placing the rosebud in the purse and taking *both* gifts back with him.

Wellesley often admitted that he was a poor scholar, and that school gave him no pleasure. Love of books did not come until he was in his middle years and he often insisted that the acute scholarship shown by some of his children was the gift of their mother who, from childhood, showed an aptitude for literature, music and languages. Wellesley was happier with horses and dogs, and his understanding of them finds confirmation in an early memory.

His father was given to hard drinking. On market days young Wellesley had to take over the reins with one hand while, with the other, he helped to keep his father from falling out of the trap.

While Wellesley was a boarder at Kilkenny College, Alice was a boarder at a school in Dublin. A close friendship developed between Alice and a girl who was probably a day pupil, since she lived in Dublin. Her name was Charlotte Pim and, though they did not know it at the time, their friendship and that of their parents which opened the Pim home in Alma Place to Alice Grahame, was to have far reaching effects on their lives and that of Wellesley Bailey.

By the time the Bailey boys were in their teens, the in-word had changed from "famine" to "emigration" and "Go west or south young man" became a familiar answer to Ireland's population problem. Families saved and scrimped in spite of the hard conditions which prevailed, so that sons and daughters showing promise could find a new and more secure life in England, or in one of the many colonies which were opening up in the expanding Empire of the young Queen Victoria. Between 1847 and 1852, 1,200,000 people, mostly young men, left Ireland to seek fame and fortune overseas.

Christopher Bailey obtained a commission in the army and sailed for India with the 11th Infantry Regiment, ultimately becoming a Colonel. Alfred also joined the army but was content to serve in the ranks as a Guardsman in the Carabiniers. The youngest son James Andrew stayed on the estate with the family, becoming, as Wellesley afterwards said, "the most Irish of all the family."

Wellesley showed no desire for the army or for the home estate. His thoughts turned instead to the new and romantic discovery of gold in the Australian outback.

In 1849 Edmund Hargreaves had found gold in California, and he remembered seeing similar geological formations while surveying in Australia. Returning, he went back over his old survey grounds and was immediately successful. Within a few years thousands of prospectors bought mining rights in Bendigo, Ballarat and Castlemane. The gold rush was on, with hordes of emigrants coming from the four corners of the world with only one thing in common— a desire to find gold, the fabled key to security and affluence. To encourage emigration, and to balance the influx of convicts and debtors who had been compulsorily transported to Australia from 1786 until 1853, the government offered cheap land-rights and a free passage for emigrants under 30 —a concession which must have appealed to the 20-year-old Wellesley as he pondered his future prospects. His decision made, Wellesley Bailey crossed the Irish Sea and made his way to London, probably tasting for the first time the new joys of rail travel which was linking all the larger towns and cities in a network of steam locomotion.

Chapter II

PIONEERS! O PIONEERS

*O you youths, western youths,
So impatient, full of action, ful of manly pride
and friendship;
Plain I see you, western youths! see you
tramping with the foremost,
Pioneers! O Pioneers.*

Walt Whitman

At the time Wellesley Bailey sailed for Australia, the full-rigged clipper ships were still operating the emigrant routes between Britain and the colonies. Two of them can still be seen as survivors of the great sailing era—the *Cutty Sark* in London, and the *Carrick*, ex-*City of Adelaide*, in Glasgow. The latter carried emigrants from the U.K. to Australia, once making a record trip from London to Adelaide in 65 days.

Until 1894, when Tower Bridge was built, shipping could not come into the heart of the city of London, and Gravesend was the dock area from which most travellers left for their long journey to the Antipodes. From London Bridge the emigrants were carried by a fleet of small steamers and wherries to the ocean going vessels.

An interesting ilustration of emigrant embarkation at this time is to be found in Ford Madox Brown's painting *The Last of England*, now in the Tate Gallery, London. The painting, finished in 1855, was inspired by the departure from Gravesend of the sculptor Thomas Woolner and his wife, *en route* for Australia.

The artist used himself, his wife and child, as his models, and the picture reflects in moving and tender tones the feeling of the traveller, taking his last look at the homeland.

"This picture", wrote the artist, "is in the truest sense historical. It treats of the great Emigration Movement which attained its culminating point in the 1860s. I have, in order to present the parting scene in its fullest tragic development, singled out a couple from the middle classes, high enough through education and refinement to appreciate all they are now giving up".

Madox Brown depicted the scene in words as well as in oils, painting a morbid, even sinister picture of the plight of the emigrants:

> *The last of England O'er the sea, my dear,*
> *Our homes to seek amid Australian fields,*
> *Us, not our million-acred island yields*
> *The space to dwell in. Thrust out, forced to hear*
> *Low ribaldry from sots, and share rough cheer*
> *From rudely-natured men* . . . . . .

The smoke from a myriad coal fires, the continuous belching of hundreds of factory chimneys, and the steamy smoke of the early locomotives, combined with the damp sea-fog which drifted in from the North Sea and the English Channel to produce the acrid "pea-souper" known and feared by residents and travellers alike.

Often ships were held up in their berths for many days so it is not surprising that we have Wellesley Bailey's account of the fog which kept him in Gravesend over the week-end following embarkation. The fog did have one good and far-reaching effect upon him. It reminded the young traveller of the promise he had made to Alice Grahame that whenever possible he would attend Church, even though he had told her before leaving Ireland, that whilst he respected her faith, he could not share it.

The Parish Church of St. George's, which stands near the quay at Gravesend, was built in 1731, after the disastrous fire of 1727 which destroyed its predecessor and a good deal of the dock area. It is chiefly known as the burial place of the ill-fated Indian Princess, Pocahantas, though it would be remembered by most emigrants as the last English landmark they saw as their vessel left Gravesend for destinations across the sea.

Whether it was St. George's Church, or the small Fishermen's Church of St. Andrew's, which Wellesley attended, we cannot be sure. What we do know is that he was greatly moved by the experience for when he returned to the ship he went down to his cabin and knelt down, offering a prayer of devout consecration and committing his life to God in whatever paths the Lord might lead.

Of the voyage to Australia, which began on Tuesday, August 28th, 1866, Wellesley Bailey left no record, but a contemporary traveller wrote a very idealized account of a similar journey, from which we may gauge his feelings:

"Beautiful and interesting is the sight presented every evening . . . The noble vessel with its beautiful tapering spars sustaining aloft her snow white wings, which are filled by the freshening breeze, rushes through the waters like a thing of life, dividing the heavy billows with its sharp prow, and covering its bows with foam like feathers on the breast of a gigantic inhabitant of upper air. The full moon, meanwhile, looks down with unclouded effulgence converting the waters into silver and rendering visible the foamy crests of the far-off billows. Around us are our companions, pilgrims in a double sense — pilgrims for a time in the world whose waters they now sail so speedily over, and pilgrims seeking a better country ere they leave this sphere for ever".

Many emigrants had a less idyllic view of the ocean for there were scores of unknown hazards to face. In the very year of Wellesley's journey the steamer *London,* bound for Australia, foundered in the Bay of Biscay with a loss of two hundred and twenty three people. Ships of this type usually had three decks, a spar or upper deck, a main deck and a between deck. There were many regulations to be followed by the emigrants such as which decks could be used, and what facilities could be obtained by the various classes of passenger, and we may be sure that the young man made the most of his opportunities for meeting and learning from people on board.

Arriving in Australia, Wellesley Bailey joined the great army of prospectors making for the new diggings—a cosmopolitan and motley group who, like him, had surrendered their ties with the old world to seek fame and fortune in the new speculative world of gold. From the Americas, Europe and even the Far East, thousands joined the trek, each believing that while others were failing in their search for wealth, they would succeed. Alas, very soon Wellesley Bailey had to realize that there was no future for him in the goldfields. He listened to the stories of alternative and less crowded opportunities which awaited the really bold adventurer, and soon he was one of a group making for New Zealand. After years of uneasy settlements and prolonged negotiations, Governor Grey had proclaimed peace with the Maori tribes and groups of settlers were being invited to take over holdings of the land. Small properties of twenty to thirty acres could be planted as orchards, fenced in as paddocks and stockyards, or given over to grazing, and these holdings, together with materials for the building of a house, were offered for a sum of four or five hundred pounds, with stocks of sheep and horses readily available.

It all seemed too good to be true, and, alas for many emigrants who participated, this is precisely what it proved to be. Keen and enthusiastic as the young adventurers were, they came down to earth physically as well as metaphorically when they took over their lots and began turning them into miniature utopias. To break-in wild horses, and prepare them for riding the sheep ranges, proved a death-defying operation. The unbroken animal would be allowed into a central paddock, lunging and bucking whenever anyone so much as approached with a halter, and even when that move was succesful the powerful horse could drag rope and holder along the dusty track as the steed careered round and round in a frenzy of fear and malice. Only when the horse wearied of its struggle would a rough-rider mount, holding on to the mane and halter until the man was thrown, or the horse was mastered and led into the stabling area. Even greater hazards were the terrible bush fires which could wipe out in a few hours the work of many months, destroying stock, homestead and holding, in their ferocity.

As we know, Wellesley Bailey had been used to the horses of his native Ireland, and in later days, when he so often travelled on horseback over the plains and foothills of India, he must have remembered gratefully the lessons he had learned in the stock-riding paddocks of New Zealand.

Once again, however, young Wellesley felt that he had made a mistake for he was no more successful with the wild horses than he had been with the gold digging.

Still wanting to justify the impulse which had brought him so many thousands of miles, he decided to go on to New Caledonia, a Pacific Island group 1,500 miles East of Queensland.

In 1842 France had formally annexed the Marquesas

Islands, to which they subsequently added New Caledonia and Tahiti. The rugged grandeur of the islands could not fail to impress the young Irishman with their high peaks, thick forests and green plains, surrounded by atolls enclosing lagoons which shimmered in the sunlight until they looked like the setting of a gigantic necklace, but, for all their beauty, the islands were no earthly paradise. The heavy storms turned the atolls into an inferno in which a plantation or homestead could disappear in a night leaving no trace of human endeavour, or life.

New Caledonia belonged to the Melanesian group of islands and the nationals, as the name of the group implied, were of negroid stock and quickly adapted themselves to life with the settlers, even though many of the former were exploited, being kidnapped for work in the forests and plantations.

The presence of small missionary groups from Europe, who followed in the wake of the early settlers, must have been a reminder to Wellesley Bailey of his own vow of consecration, made so sincerely on the night of his embarkation at Gravesend, and his prayer became an urgent plea for guidance and wise judgement. He could only feel that Australia, New Zealand and New Caledonia were but halting places in his search for the right paths of service. He was not afraid of hard work or tough circumstances but, at the least, he wanted to be assured that there was an end product to his endeavours which was above mercenary gain.

Reluctantly, he decided that the only hope lay in retracing his steps so he sailed for Ireland and home.

It was not the homecoming he had anticipated when he had left Ireland fired by lofty ambition, but he was humble enough to realize that he had mistaken his vocation, and he must have envied his brothers their sense of security and assurance.

Chapter III

A NEW BEGINNING

Where shall I go Lord? where shall I go?
Wisdom to guide me Thou wilt bestow;
Help me to go, Lord, where Thou dost lead,
Trusting Thy promise, "Grace for all need".
                                   Flora Kirkland

When the way ahead is unclear, there is a threefold guide which helps to prepare the heart, mind and will to find and accept the new way. If our own thoughts after prayer, the advice of trusted friends and the force of circumstances coincide, we are not likely to be far from the will of God.

These three avenues of experience meant a good deal to Wellesley Bailey throughout his life, but at no point were they more important than in the new waiting period in Ireland. He accepted the disciplines imposed upon him by the situation, and was glad to listen to the advice of his loved ones both at home and overseas. It was, in fact, from India that he received a clear indication of the next move, by an invitation he received from his oldest brother, Christopher, who was now serving as an officer with the British Army, at Faizabad, in Oudh (now Uttar Pradesh), North India.

Christopher suggested that Wellesley should join him in Oudh with a view to securing a commission in the North West Police, and since a prerequisite for the post was a knowledge of Hindustani, Christopher suggested that his brother should have tuition in the language at Faizabad.

Once again he set sail for distant shores, but shortly after Wellesley's arrival in India his brother's regiment, the 11th Infantry Brigade, was moved away, and Christopher was ordered home, so a suitable lodging was sought for his younger brother.

The Rev. Mr. Reuther, of the Church Missionary Society, was living in an old Muslim memorial tomb which had been adapted to serve as a missionary home, and he was only too pleased to offer hospitality to Wellesley, who never forgot his kindness. Writing during a later missionary journey he said: "In the afternoon Miss Fallon very kindly drove me out to see some of the familiar old places. I saw the old tomb, used for many years as the C.M.S. Mission House, where under the charm of dear old Mr. Reuther's influence, I received my first drawings towards missionary work. I saw also the little prayer-room where I spent many a happy half-hour with some of the Christian men of the 11th Foot, and where I made my first attempts at speaking in public".

Wellesley Bailey was now twenty-three and, for the first time, he felt he knew where he was going, and why!

All his experiences in Ireland, Australia, New Zealand and New Caledonia were seen as good missionary training; and every gift and talent was sure to find a place in God's loving purpose for him.

Academically speaking, his only qualification for missionary service was a knowledge of Hindustani but, armed only with this, he applied to the American Presbyterian Mission for service in one of their schools in North India. To his great joy, and probably to his great surprise, he was accepted and was asked to report to the Staff at Ambala City in the Punjab for service as a teacher in their mission school.

The leader at Ambala was the Rev. J. H. Morrison, D.D., who later became known throughout the world for his sponsorship of the Universal Week of Prayer, which still unites many Protestant Christians in intercessory prayer during the first full week of each year.

Wellesley Bailey joined Dr. Morrison and his son in the autumn of 1869 and quickly settled down to the routine of an Indian Mission centre, teaching some of the 400 children during the day and assisting with general missionary work in the evening.

After giving the missionary recruit a complete month to settle down, Dr. Morrison introduced him to a side of the work of which he was completely ignorant. This was the work Dr. Morrison was doing for forty leprosy beggars of Ambala who were housed in a small asylum not far from the mission compound; we will let Wellesley tell the story of his first visit in his own way:

"To my surprise I found it was but a little way off, just on the other side of the road from my house, yet perhaps numbers had, like myself, passed by in utter ignorance that within a stone's throw of the public highway men and women suffering from the dread disease of leprosy were being sheltered and kindly cared for. The asylum consisted of three rows of huts under some trees. In front of one row the inmates had assembled for worship. They were in all stages of the malady, very terrible to look upon, with a sad, woebegone expression on their faces—a look of utter helplessness. I almost shuddered, yet I was at the time fascinated, and I felt, if ever there was a Christ-like work in the world it was to go among these poor sufferers and bring to them the consolation of the Gospel". When Dr. Morrison saw that his young colleague, far from being repulsed by what he saw and heard, was attracted to the work among the leprosy sufferers, he encouraged him to take an interest in their welfare and soon offered to make it over to him so that it became one of Wellesley Bailey's personal responsibilities. This brought great joy to Dr. Morrison, whose health was failing, and he was able to take a much needed rest in the hills, secure in the knowledge that his suffering friends would not be forgotten.

"I visited them regularly", confided Wellesley Bailey in a letter home, "and found my visits very much appreciated. Little by little a feeling of confidence was established. I found that they were by no means as dull as might have been expected, and that they had already a considerable grasp on the truth of the Gospel—they had been well instructed by Dr. Morrison, and it was bearing fruit".

A further seal was set on the young missionary's work when some of the leprosy sufferers came forward for Christian baptism on profession of their new-found faith, convincing him that "their first and greatest need was the Gospel, and that it would indeed prove to them 'the power of God unto Salvation', completely changing their lives and their outlook on life, and giving them something to look forward to even in this life, but especially in that which is to come; and that it brought to them very real comfort in the midst of their dreadful sufferings".

He was soon to find that taking Christian teaching to the sufferers was not enough, and he began to engage in correspondence with missionaries and others who were exercised about the problems brought by leprosy. Though, initially, it had seemed that visitation and ministry were all he could bring to the task, he now began to take an interest in social hygiene; attending to their living accommodation, clothing, sanitation and even simple medication.

"Up to that time," he later wrote, "little had been done for them (I speak specially of India). There were here and there what one might term refuges, known by various names, sometimes 'poorhouses', sometimes 'asylums', *etc*. Some of these consisted of buildings erected at Government or Municipal expense, and generally supported by Municipalities with the aid of help from the outside public, largely the

European element". The work at Ambala fell into this category, being supported by the municipality and the donations of kindly disposed friends of Dr. Morrison.

Wellesley's letters home began to contain more and more references to his work for the leprosy sufferers of Ambala, and, as he had been for about three years, engaged to be married to Alice Grahame, his childhood friend, she shared his letters with her three Dublin friends, the Misses Pim.

His growing interest in leprosy work brought with it a desire to see what others were doing for their welfare. He travelled to Subathu, near Simla, to see Dr. John Newton who in 1868 had built a small asylum which still continues as one of the hospitals of The Leprosy Mission.

Dr. Newton was a missionary of the American Presbyterian Mission; on his arrival at Subathu, he found a few leprosy sufferers living in a small poorhouse. Of them he wrote to Wellesley Bailey, saying that no class of the people had so moved his pity than the numerous leprosy sufferers who lived in the hills around Subathu and he felt sure that most of the families in the district had at least one member suffering from the disease.

Another early benefactor of Indian leprosy sufferers was Ensign (afterwards Sir Henry) Ramsay. Stationed with his regiment in 1835 in the hilly district around Almora, the young officer was greatly moved by the destitute leprosy victims he saw squatting by the roadside or struggling along with the aid of makeshift crutches. Not satisfied with the little charitable gifts he bestowed in passing, the Ensign used his own money to pay for the erection of a few rough huts built from the stones which lay around in abundance. Shelter from the elements and treatment as human beings did more for the sufferers than could ever have been expected, and from the little colony a leprosy hospital was established which, like Subathu, continues its links with The Leprosy Mission to this day.

William Carey, the pioneer missionary of the Baptists, wrote in a letter dated September 1812, "Last week I saw the burning of a poor leprous man. I got there too late, as he was lifeless before I arrived. I find that it is very common practice here. The poor man was well enough to go about himself. They had dug a pit about ten cubits deep, in which they made a fire. After all was prepared, the poor man rolled himself into it. But, when he felt the fire, he prayed to get out, but his sister and another relation thrust him down again, and he was burned to death! What horrible murder!" His biographer, Adam Smith, says of the incident's influence on the missionary: "Carey never rested till a leprosy hospital was established in Calcutta, near the centre of the Church Missionary Society's work!" The fourth issue of the Serampore magazine of Dr. Marshman speaks of the rejoicing over Kali Sankar Ghosal's offer of the land and money for the founding of a leprosy asylum, and a Brahmin convert of William Carey's built a small asylum for leprosy sufferers near Allahabad, about 1830.

Inspired by examples like this, Wellesley Bailey was constrained to work and think and pray, not only for the leprosy sufferers of Ambala, but for *all* such sufferers everywhere.

To his intense joy, his fiancée was sympathetic with all his ideals and he felt the need to have her share his work more intimately. At his urgent request, Alice Grahame left her home at Blackrock, in Ireland, and sailed for Bombay, where they were married in the Cathedral on October 13th, 1871. She was his helpmate in all his labours until her death in 1924. For all the fifty-three years Alice Bailey was counsellor and colleague to her husband and, when their marriage was blessed with children, she imprinted on their lives those facets of character and conduct which had attracted Wellesley to her during their youth. In education and culture she brought to the work of Wellesley Bailey a gift of organisation and stability which was to be a strong tower of support as their shared ministry developed. Her children and grandchildren remember her as a woman of great sensibility and, though never physically strong, she more than made up for it in mental vigour and courage.

From Ambala, Wellesley Bailey was posted to Ludhiana but he continued to pray for the sufferers of Ambala and sought to do for other sufferers what he had done for them.

Chapter IV

A MISSION IS BORN

*If I stoop
Into a dark tremendous sea of cloud
It is but for a time; I press God's lamp
Close to my breast, its splendour soon or late
Will pierce the gloom.*

Robert Browning

Although Mrs. Bailey greatly appreciated the opportunity of serving with her husband in North India, the life and work there brought health hazards, and Wellesley was warned in the Autumn of 1873 that he must take his wife back to Ireland. They arrived home at the end of the year but as so often happens in life, the seeming destruction of their plans led to even greater advances.

The letters from India had proved so challenging to Alice Bailey's friends, the Misses Isabella, Charlotte and Jane Pim, that the presence of Wellesley and Alice made it possible for them to have first-hand reports of what was going on at Ambala, Ludhiana and elsewhere. This was followed by a drawing-room meeting in the Alma Place home of the Pim family for invited guests, and a more public meeting on September 6th, 1874, at the Friends Meeting House at Monkstown. Wellesley was only too pleased to share his experiences in this way; all who heard him were moved by his sincerity and compassion, as he pleaded the cause of the leprosy sufferers he had learned to love in North India.

We cannot be sure just how the seed sown germinated so quickly; the important fact is that it *did* grow into a desire for service, linking the praying group at home with the serving group on the Field. Touched by what they had heard the friends in Dublin undertook to raise £30 a year so that provision might be made for further help to be given to the needy sufferers. By the end of the year they had raised not £30 but nearly £600 and the question they asked was one of stewardship! For what purpose had this large sum of money been entrusted to them? They had certainly not considered setting up a new missionary society but they must, at least, organize the work in such a way that more victims of leprosy might find shelter and care.

Miss Charlotte Pim became Honorary Secretary of the support group; Wellesley Bailey assured them that he would be able to pass on the money donated to those who were actually giving to leprosy sufferers the kind of help which he had been able to give at Ambala.

To help maintain and extend the interest of friends in Ireland Wellesley Bailey wrote down the substance of his Dublin addresses in a small sixteen-page pamphlet which he entitled *Lepers in India*. It was reprinted constantly during the years which followed. It was reviewed in missionary magazines and the booklet's influence continued to grow, earning for it the name of "the penny beggar". Although it was his first excursion into print it was a model of factual presentation, emotional appeal, and practical challenge, leaving the Christian reader in no doubt as to where his responsibility lay.

Mr. and Mrs. Bailey returned to India in December, 1874, under the auspices of the Church of Scotland Mission and were posted to Chamba. At once they began to use the Dublin gifts to bring care and the consolation of the Gospel to such leprosy sufferers as they found in the district around Chamba. They built for them a group of simple huts where the leprosy victims quickly settled into a new colony of fellowship beyond their wildest dreams. It was the first of the Leprosy Homes to be built by the new Mission. As this venture did not use up all the funds entrusted to him, Wellesley remembered his friend Dr. John Newton, and wrote to him offering financial help so that a few more leprosy victims might be taken into his asylum at Subathu.

Dr. Newton was overwhelmed by the offer and his answer read: "Whilst walking here from K- I had been turning over and over in my mind what to do to get funds to meet the wants of these people. I have eleven in the poorhouse, but there are hundreds in this region, and I have been compelled to refuse admission to many most urgent cases. If you are willing to entrust to me the stewardship of the fund, I, for my part, will thankfully accept it, and will look to the Lord Jesus to enable me to discharge it faithfully".

Among the five patients he was able to help was a woman named Delphi who, with her two children, had begged her way ninety miles over the Himalayas to seek shelter at Subathu.

Soon requests came from other missionaries concerned for leprosy sufferers in the midst of their other duties and the Baileys were only too pleased to help, using the funds which began to come regularly from Dublin.

The Church of Scotland Home and Foreign Missionary Record reprinted copious extracts from *Lepers in India* and commended it to their own readers, supplying addresses to which further gifts for the work could be sent.

After outlining the events which led to the writing of the pamphlet Wellesley Bailey had written: "Many people are startled when we first broach the subject of Leprosy. 'Why', they say, 'I thought no such thing existed nowadays. You don't mean to say that you have lepers in India like those we read of in the Bible?' But it is even so; not only in India but almost in every country in the world." The author then gave a pen picture of the suffering he had seen at Ambala and other places and indicated the ways in which he had been able to help the sufferers.

Then came his appeal for further help, under the heading *"What can be done"*, in which he pointed out that for as little as £5 an adult victim could be cared for in an asylum; the amount was correspondingly less for a child. "Now what I propose", he went on, "is that Churches, Sabbath Schools, working parties, and individuals should take upon themselves the support of one or more lepers! and *guarantee* the amount necessary. Those unable to support *one* need not therefore be debarred from participation. They might undertake to pay half, a fourth, or *any* part of the support of one, only it will be well if, whatever they give, they give *regularly*. The *smallest* subscription and donation will be gladly received, so that every one may help a little."

"Help a little" they did, and it was found necessary to issue *Occasional Papers* each half-year giving the list of contributions received. *Occasional Paper No. 1* (Jan-May 1875) gave news of the work at Chamba and Subathu but although the list of donors contained about four hundred names and a number of "Anon" gifts, Wellesley Bailey confessed "to a feeling of disappointment, when I observed absent from that list the names of many whom I believed would have been amongst the first to come forward", adding: "I would not feel justified in commencing this work on any very large scale, until I know what amount of permanent support we are likely to have. People may say this is want of faith. It may be so; but I do not feel it to be so. What I feel is that we must go little by little, step by step, as the Lord leads and not rush ahead of his leading, and then find ourselves in difficulties. It would be a very serious thing to collect a lot of these helpless ones, get them to look to us for support, and then afterwards find that we could not keep so many, and have to turn some of them adrift again. I know with some these views may not find favour; but then everyone is entitled to his own, and these are mine". "Will friends kindly bear in mind", he cautioned, "that I am not *solely* a missionary to the lepers, although sometimes I almost wish I were, but that I am connected with a society, and that my first duty is to attend to their work (I venture to hope, however, that they will be willing to consider this a very important branch of it), which will, of course, give me less time to work amongst the lepers, and prevent information being collected and work set a-going so quickly as it otherwise might be".

So it was that within a year of his appointment as lay-evangelist at Chamba, Wellesley Bailey was already caught up in the bewildering search after priorities, and he knew that compassion for the leprosy sufferers was to be in the ascendancy in his life. The more he saw of the need, the more he felt impelled to meet it, if this proved possible.

Chapter V

HOW FAR CAN WE GO?

Grant us the will to fashion as we feel,
Grant us the strength to labour as we know,
Grant us the purpose, ribb'd and edged with steel,
To strike the blow.

John Drinkwater

Wellesley Bailey's chief responsibility on returning to India was, as he pointed out to his friends, the work of the Church of Scotland, whose Home Board had appointed him, and whose supporters were paying his salary and providing him with a house at Chamba. The Mission Board, meeting in July 1875, heard a report from the young missionary on his plan for opening a new school in the city and sanctioned the project, subject to his being able to find Christian teachers to staff the school. In his enthusiasm Wellesley had already got his sights on a veritable chain of such schools, and the Board had to remind him that "one good school well-equipped" was better than a number of schools with limited attendance.

In spite of his enthusiasm for the education of children in North India, his heart was still with the leprosy victims, and the following year letters were passed between the missionary and the Mission Board in an effort to ease the situation. In a minute dated October 18th, 1876 it was recorded; "Read letters of August 30th and September 12th from Mr. Bailey, Chamba, to the Correspondent, who was instructed to reply that the Committee are prepared to accept his work among lepers as work for the Committee, so long as it does not interfere with his other duties in Chamba".

Having received the goodwill of the Mission Board, Wellesley Bailey felt able to give more thought to the needs of those he now called "our lepers" and he sought to identify himself more closely with them by studying the disease patterns and the relative requirements of each group of sufferers. At this time, Dr. Newton left Subathu for a well-earned furlough and, to Wellesley's joy, Dr. J. H. Morrison, his friend from Ambala, came to supervise the work at Subathu and was able to tell him about some new treatment which was being tried out as a result of tests made in the Andaman Islands by Dr. Doughall, the Civil Surgeon in charge of a convict settlement there. Dr. Doughall had found that the progress of the disease was arrested by the application of Gurjan oil, (a resinous substance found in the Andamans), directly onto the skin of the sufferer.

At once, Mr. Bailey wrote to Dr. Doughall asking for a fifty-four gallon cask of the oil so that treatment with it could begin at Subathu! Writing home about the new treatment on December 24th 1875, he was enthusiastic though anxious that the applications should be both systematic and thorough, remarking: "In the case of convicts in the Andamans it was easily managed, as there was simply an order given that the lepers were to rub in the oil every day for a certain time, and to take the emulsion so many times, and it *had* to be obeyed; whereas in our case we cannot do that without interfering with the liberty of the subject However, we are doing the best we can to give the thing a fair trial. Oh, may our loving Father be pleased to bless our efforts!"

This extract is very revealing since it shows Wellesley Bailey's determination to use every method available for helping the sufferers. He was shocked to find that even in

Society, and Mr. Bailey's help saved the work from embarrassment if not disaster since, in Mr. Budden's estimation, "it averted the necessity of any curtailment in the operations of the asylum, and called forth lively gratitude in the hearts of all connected with it".

Although the tensions concerning his activities were unrelieved, Mr. and Mrs. Bailey continued their work at Wazirabad. However, Mrs. Bailey's health failed to improve and, in April 1881, he requested that they be permitted to have a furlough from January 1882. In reply the members of the Church of Scotland Foreign Mission Board acceded to his request but informed him, "that in the present circumstances they would not be able to send him out again". At the request of the Board the Baileys stayed on at Wazirabad until April 1882, when they returned to Dublin with their family, still very uncertain of the way ahead!

Looking back over the eleven years they had served together in India, there was so much that gave them encouragement. With the backing of the Dublin friends they had built and sustained a leprosy asylum in Chamba, and given support to established work at Subathu, Ambala and Almora but, more important, they had gained first-hand knowledge of the wider problems of leprosy in India and were known to an increasing number of missionaries and municipal officers who received their help and encouragement, as "friends of the lepers". At home they had a closely knit fellowship of supporters in Ireland, chiefly in Dublin, with individual supporters in England and Scotland, but they realised that their homecoming and subsequent resignation from the Church of Scotland Foreign Mission Board must lead to a reappraisal of the whole situation. The death of his dear friend and colleague the Rev. John Newton M.D. of Subathu made Mr. Bailey realise the need for continuity of administration, knowing that "whilst God removes the workers, he still pain could enter, and the young man testified his trust in Christ saying, "I can thank God for this terrible disease, for it has been the means of bringing me to Him".

Another publication to appear in 1878 was the first of the long line of Annual Reports which has continued to the present time.

Mr. and Mrs. Bailey returned to India filled with uncertainty about the future. Meanwhile, at the headquarters of the Church of Scotland Foreign Mission Board the question of the exact location of their future work was still under discussion.

In July the Board were informed "that on account of Mrs. Bailey's health it was not deemed prudent that they should go to Pangi, and that in consequence they had gone to Bhandel". The December minutes read: "Future location of Mr. Bailey to Wazirabad considered, also the suggestion that he might go temporarily to Darjeeling to take charge of the work there until the new missionary arrived".

In March 1879 it was reported that the "services of Mr. Bailey were not required in Darjeeling and therefore transfer to Wazirabad recommended" but the decision was not at all pleasing to Wellesley Bailey and urgent letters of protest from him followed in quick succession. The Board was adamant that he should go where he was directed. Though disappointed, Wellesley Bailey accepted the authority of the Mission Board and continued his work in the school at Wazirabad, while still increasing his contacts in North India with individuals and groups engaging in leprosy work. Subathu still had pride of place but he gave continued support to Ambala where he had first become interested in the plight of leprosy sufferers, and to Almora, where leprosy work had been established in 1849. For many years the work at Almora, commenced by Sir Henry Ramsay, had been under the care of the Rev. J. H. Budden of the London Missionary

Mr. and Mrs. Bailey were content to leave the issue with the Mission Board. That body, meeting on September 18th, 1877 decided to transfer the Baileys to Pangi with effect from December 18th. Wellesley was a born fighter and the controversy over his work at Chamba and Subathu (to which he travelled whenever possible), only served to strengthen his convictions but, to a person as sensitive as his wife, the tensions were becoming intolerable and her health began to suffer. Pending further consultation with regard to their ultimate posting, the Baileys were offered a furlough and were thus able to be present in Dublin for the formation of the first Committee of The Mission to Lepers in India.

With the increasing number of subscribers at home and the growth of the contacts in India, the Misses Pim and their local group of helpers were in need of a Committee to which they could turn for help and advice. The number of leprosy sufferers being helped by the Mission was now approaching 100, while contributions for the previous year were close to £900 and it was clear that a more ordered form of administration was called for. Miss Charlotte E. Pim was confirmed in her appointment as Honorary Secretary with Mr. Graves S. Eves as Honorary Treasurer, and a committee of seven was formed, with three men and three women serving with Wellesley himself.

The little booklet *Lepers in India* continued to be the main promotional instrument, but it was now joined by an 8-page tract entitled, *Rejoicing in Hope or, The Happy Leper*. It was a story told by Wellesley Bailey of a young European who had contracted leprosy in India and was visited by Mr. Bailey at the request of the hospital physician.

Thinking Wellesley was a doctor, the patient's marred face opened into a pleasant smile as he said, eagerly, "Do you think I shall get better?" The visitor could only counsel faith and hope in another realm where neither disease or places like Ambala the inmates were receiving no medical care at all, and he observed with regret the worsening of their condition since the previous visit. "While they were well cared for", he wrote, "had good food and clothing, and comfortable houses to live in, the disease seemed to hold complete sway over them" whereas, at Subathu, it seemed that the disease was held in check.

The Times of India, for October 19th, 1875, carried two long articles on the subject of leprosy in India and one of them quoted the writer as complaining: "neither religion, nor benevolence, nor enlightened selfishness takes thought of them. No priest of any faith, no man or woman goes amongst them to give material or moral consolation of any kind, they are abandoned of God and man".

In answer to this charge of indifference by Christians Wellesley Bailey reported on leprosy care being given at the Jamsetjee Hospital where there was a leprosy ward which he had visited, at which he had shared in a service taken by an Indian Christian worker, Mr. Bewazu. The second article in *The Times* contained a plea for a leprosy asylum for Bombay's leprosy sufferers, 169 of whom were known to the authorities, and Mr. Bailey supported the appeal for this and other groups of sufferers.

By his reading, his correspondence and his visits to the missionary centres, Wellesley Bailey was building up a store of information which continued to challenge him but, though he had the approval of the Home Committee to do what leprosy work he could fit in with his normal missionary duties, there were members of Staff in North India who thought the young missionary was undertaking too much work on behalf of leprosy sufferers. One missionary in particular, Dr. Hutchinson, informed the Home Committee of his fears and there was much correspondence, often acrimonious, between North India and the Board's offices in Edinburgh. As usual carries on the work"—words quoted by Mr. Bailey in the sixth Annual Report. Dr. Newton's widow nobly took up the work of her late husband, helped by the Rev. D. Herron, and the Dublin Committee were quick to assure them that the Mission's help would continue.

"Whatever happens to any of us," Mr. and Mrs. Bailey insisted, "the work amongst the leprosy sufferers must continue." To them it was unthinkable that the work, begun as a commission from God, should suffer because they were not themselves able to supervise it in India. The Mission which had begun in prayer must be cradled in prayer until the Lord's will became clear. The 1882 furlough in Dublin was to give Wellesley Bailey just the opportunity and challenge he needed to prepare for the next step.

Chapter VI

IN STEP WITH THE MASTER

One step I see before me; 'Tis all I need to see,
The light of heaven more brightly shines, when earth's
  illusions flee;
And sweetly through the silence comes His loving
  "Follow Me".
So on I go not knowing, I would not if I might;
I'd rather walk in the dark with God, than go alone in the
  light;
I'd rather walk by faith with Him, than go alone by sight.

Mary G. Brainerd

It must have seemed to Wellesley Bailey, as he looked back over the past two decades, that his way of life was hedged about to an alarming degree. Each time he took a step forward it had at first seemed that his life's work had opened out, but on at least five occasions he had found not an open road but a *cul-de-sac*. He was now thirty-six and his travels had already gained him experience in a number of widely different fields but it was the need of the leprosy sufferers which had charged his life with the greatest dynamic. The group of Dublin supporters were appalled at the thought that they might lose his leadership but, on the other hand, they could not see their way to offering him a full-time post where, until now, all the work had been honorary. He was however, invited to become Secretary of the Scottish Association of the Zenana Bible and Medical Mission, which operated from Edinburgh, and it was arranged that he should be free to continue to serve The Mission to Lepers in India as one of the two Honorary Secretaries and Treasurers for the Mission's overseas activities, the other being the Rev. J. H. Budden, of Almora.

The Bailey family moved to 17, Glengyle Terrace, Edinburgh, and Wellesley threw himself into his new duties with zest, glad to find that the post offered many new links with India.

The Zenana Bible and Medical Mission was formed in the 1850's as a result of the reports sent from India by John Fordyce, a Scottish missionary who pleaded the cause of India's women who were, in his words, "morally polluted, mentally benighted and, relative to man, cruelly degraded" because of the tragic social system which banished them to the zenana, or women's quarters of the educated classes. English ladies volunteered to go to India as teachers with a special concern for the wives and daughters of educated nationals. Robert Johnson, an elderly Edinburgh resident, who had been in business in Patna, initially gave £25, and later gave £150 a year, to start a Patna Zenana Mission. This project became the special responsibility of the Edinburgh Z.B.M.M. Within a year no less than thirty-three zenanas were open and a small school "for the pooorer sort" had been opened. By the end of 1887 there were seventy-three zenanas open and four schools, all operating in spite of the most violent opposition.

The Patna missionaries, doubtless encouraged by advisers like Wellesley Bailey, were among the first Z.B.M.M. workers to plead for medical services to go hand in hand with the educational work and *The Times* of London published a leader on the need for Medical Missions for Indian women, based on an article in the *Indian Female Evangelist*. It urged the government to support in every way those who were willing to go and help their needy sisters, but, as the Z.B.M.M.

pointed out, there were few women qualified in medicine and there were few inducements to call them to India. Under the patronage of the Queen herself and Lady Dufferin, wife of the Viceroy of India, a group of interested people founded the "National Association for supplying Female Medical Aid to the Women of India", shortened, understandably enough, to "The Lady Dufferin Fund". The Vicereine's interest in medical missions was to have a lasting effect upon leprosy work when she became the first Patroness of The Mission to Lepers in India.

Side by side with his Zenana work, Wellesley Bailey continued his links with the leprosy service he had begun in India, and shared the home administration of The Mission to Lepers in India with Miss Charlotte Pim and Mr. Graves S. Eves. More than a hundred leprosy victims were now supported by the Dublin Committee and fresh appeals were coming in from areas beyond the centres formerly helped. Dr. Neve, a C.M.S. medical missionary working at Srinagar in Kashmir, sought help for the leprosy sufferers under his care explaining that he was trying to bring relief to some victims by "nerve stretching", a surgical technique he had developed whilst allowing leprosy patients into his general hospital; both ideas being far in advance of most leprosy workers at that time.

Increased giving from supporters in England came at a time when new work on the field called for greater benevolence. Two names came into the report which were to have lasting significance—namely, Brighton, and Gossner's Mission, the latter a German Missionary Society working in India. A copy of Mr. Bailey's booklet *Lepers in India* came into the hands of a Major-General Hoste, C.B.E., but it remained unnoticed for almost eight years. In 1882, he found it in a drawer and took it with him when he went to address a class of girls in Brighton led by Miss Jane Mohun. After the meeting, the speaker left the tract with his hostess. Reading it led her to found the "Brighton Auxiliary" of The Mission to Lepers in India. The first gift of the Brighton friends was accompanied by a promise to send one hundred pounds annually, and the gift and the promise were at once passed on to the Rev. F. Hahn, of Gossner's Evangelical Mission who was stationed at Lohardaga in Bihar. Mr. Hahn had written to Mr. Bailey in 1881 asking for his advice on the care of leprosy sufferers and it was a great surprise to him when Mr. Bailey offered to assist him, with the help of the Brighton friends, in the erection of a small "leper asylum" The German missionary wrote in 1844:

"This was a new idea to me, but believing it was the Lord who had thus called me to serve Him by more special work among those afflicted with leprosy, I began at once. Having gathered the necessary information, I corresponded with the authorities of my Society, and so wonderfully did God prepare the way, that in February last the building of an Asylum was commenced. This branch of the work is carried on under the auspices of the Brighton Auxiliary of The Mission to Lepers in India, whilst the Committee of Gossner's Mission Society at Berlin has undertaken the superintendence of the institution". From the same area as Lohardaga, another cry came which was to lead to the founding of the largest Home and Hospital of The Mission to Lepers in India, at Purulia. As is often the case in such ventures the beginnings were very simple. Writing of the work at Lohardaga, Mr. Hahn told Mr. Bailey the distressing story of a group of leprosy sufferers at Purulia. A charitably disposed district officer having seen the desperate plight of some leprosy beggars, authorised the building of a few simple huts on the northern outskirts of the town. Here, the leprosy victims lived in peace until the district officer was replaced by a man who considered them a nuisance. He issued an order for their huts to be burned down and for them to be compulsorily sent away to other areas where, of course, they were not received. The upshot was that they filtered back to Purulia, and encamped under the trees which marked their former home. Here, they were visited by the Rev. Henry Uffmann, a German missionary of the Gossner Mission, and a friend of the Rev. F. Hahn. Mr. Uffmann had cause to fear leprosy for his own daughter, Maria, had contracted the disease before she was eight years of age. At the age of thirteen she died in Germany as a result of her illness.

In Purulia, Mr. Uffmann did what he could for the homeless sufferers and, on the advice of Mr. Hahn, he wrote to Wellesley Bailey asking for help.

At a Committee Meeting of the Mission, held in Dublin on February 7th 1884, the Purulia situation was discussed and it was resolved that "Mr. Bailey be requested to correspond with Mr. Hahn in relation to starting a Leper Asylum at Purulia; and that our Honorary Treasurer and the Honorary Secretary be authorised to assist to the extent of £100 should Mr. Bailey be satisfied of the desirability of so assisting".

The Rev J. H. Budden of Almora returned to Britain in time to take part in the Tenth Anniversary of the Mission. For Wellesley Bailey, it was a glad reunion with his missionary colleague. Mr. Budden was able to speak about the Indian leprosy work in Dublin, Edinburgh, Brighton and other places, and everywhere the supporters were thrilled and encouraged by his first-hand reports. For thirty-three years Mr. Budden had been in charge of the asylum at Almora, and he had also travelled widely to see work in other areas of need. Mary Budden, his daughter, also addressed many meetings, speaking chiefly of the work among the children of leprosy parents which she had fostered as a pioneer project.

An indication of the growth of the work during the first decade was the formation of a Committee of Reference in

India. Among those who consented to serve on it were the Hon. Sir Henry Ramsay, C.B., K.C.S.I., of Almora: the Rev. Henry Parker (C.M.S.), of Calcutta; and the Rev. David Herron (A.P.M.) of Rawalpindi.

Thanks were expressed to Wellesley Bailey who "notwithstanding the constant pressure of other work, has done much to stir up an interest in the cause". His heart was full of thanksgiving that he had been able to see such fruit coming from ground where he had sowed the seed ten years before and he could speak with pride of a Mission whose ministry of love extended from the Himalayas to Cape Comorin."

By 1886 the work had developed so much that he was able to give up all his other work to become full-time Secretary of The Mission to Lepers in India.

Chapter VII

IN JOURNEYINGS OFT

There are who roam
To scatter seeds of life on barbarous shores.

William Wordsworth

One of the first decisions made by the Dublin Committee after the appointment of their first full-time Secretary was to suggest that Mr. and Mrs. Bailey should return to India. During a five months' stay they travelled over 9,400 miles visiting the Presidencies of Bombay, Madras and Bengal; the Central and North-West Provinces; Oudh, the Punjab, and Rajpootana and a number of the Native States.

Because of his constant study of the disease and the increasing correspondence he was undertaking with missionaries involved in the care of leprosy sufferers, Wellesley Bailey was well-equipped to undertake such a tour, and he was warmly received everywhere. Work he had previously seen was evaluated under changed conditions brought about during his four years' absence from India and he soon learned that already it was beginning to be a different India. Queen Victoria had been proclaimed Empress of India in 1877, at a magnificent ceremony in Delhi, the old capital of the Moghul emperors, and she was determined to implement, if at all possible, the policy of political justice, religious toleration and social service announced in her name at the Allahabad Durbar in November, 1858. Lord Dufferin, who with his wife had already taken an interest in leprosy work and female education since becoming Viceroy of India in 1884, was giving a lead in social reform "by seeking to break down the age-long oriental indifference of the people to the most elementary principles of sanitation, hygiene and health". Anything therefore, that Wellesley Bailey could do in relation to the problem of leprosy in India would have the ear of the Viceroy and the more enlightened Provincial and District Officers.

At the same time old prejudices were beginning to show signs of weakness, though they were far from dead. Those most closely concerned with the treatment of the disease were beginning to believe that the disease was not hereditary though it was contagious, and centres like Almora were already segregating healthy children from leprous parents in an effort to save them from contagion. The killing of leprosy sufferers had been abolished along with the burning of widows, and the time was ripe for leprosy to be treated as a disease and not a stigma.

Though there was as yet no hope of cure and rehabilitation, patients in medically supervised asylums were showing signs of progress rather than constant regression; the saving factor was the regular food supply, so that Wellesley Bailey was able to declare: "In my experience of leper asylums—now extending over a considerable number of years—I have found the physical condition of the inmates good, just in proportion to the amount of nourishing generous diet, and medical care bestowed upon them. In going the rounds of the different Leper Asylums of India, nothing strikes one so forcibly as this. Lepers require, as well as good food and clothing and kind medical care, plenty of fresh air, room to move about, good bathing accommodation, and something to occupy their minds—such as a little light gardening, or learning to read, or something of that sort."

These acute observations were the criteria by which he judged the asylums he visited and he was moved to sorrow, and even anger, when they were missing. He saw centres which left him in despair, where crowds of leprosy sufferers were huddled together in most inadequate quarters, and centres where the patients were happy, clean and comfortable. At one 'hospital', at Pallypuram, in South India, proudly proclaiming its date of founding as 1728 A.D., he found no one in charge. He found a "charity shed" at Alleppey where sufferers lay uncared for on the sandy floor, their untreated ulcers making "a truly horrible sight". Here, at Alleppey, however there was a brighter sequel for his talks with local C.M.S. workers led to the opening of a small but adequate Leprosy Home two years later.

A similar new Home followed his visit to Allahabad where, as we have seen, asylum care had been established in 1830 by one of William Carey's Brahmin converts. In 1862 a new asylum was built on a better site, a few miles east of the city, and further development took place in 1875. The Baileys arrived in Allahabad just in time to take part in the Christmas morning service at the Divinity School of the C.M.S. Later, they visited the twenty inmates in the small leper asylum and promised to supply much needed medical supplies. This initial visit was the beginning of a great tradition of leprosy service involving The Mission to Lepers and missionary groups at work in this large and important city. To the Hindu it is one of the most sacred cities in India because it is built at the site where the two great rivers Ganges and Jumna meet, a confluence bringing countless thousands of pilgrims to Allahabad year by year.

From Allahabad the traveller turned south-east and passed into Bengal where he met the Rev. P. H. Uffmann, of Purulia, whose letters concerning the leprosy beggars in the area had touched Mr. Bailey's pity. The journey from Allahabad to Purulia began by train but soon the railroad ended and in the middle of the night Mr. Bailey waited by the roadside for the *palki*, or covered litter, which was to take him on to Purulia. All the next day he was carried in the litter until, in the evening, a messenger stopped the eleven men who were carrying Mr. Bailey and his luggage, with the welcome news that refreshments prepared by Mrs. Uffmann awaited the party at a nearby guest house. Fortified with the meal the carrying party proceeded on their journey and arrived at Purulia at midnight. While the two men were together during the next three days they talked of the needs of the leprosy sufferers and marked out a site for the projected asylum, and Mr. Bailey left his host with the assurance that the cost of the asylum and its maintenance up to £100 per year would be assured by the Mission's supporters in England. From the Rev. P. H. Uffmann and his colleague, the Rev. F. Hahn, of Lohardaga, who was next on the visiting list, Wellesley Bailey learned the story of the German Gossner Mission and its work. The Gossner Evangelical Lutheran Mission, named after its founder Pastor Gossner, was organised in 1844 when it sent four missionaries to Bengal, and its success may be judged by the fact that when Mr. Bailey visited Mr. Hahn, he had 1,200 converts under his immediate care, among whom were a number of leprosy sufferers. Whilst at Lohardaga, Mr. Bailey was able to open a new Prayer-room at the asylum, the first of many he was to dedicate on his tours of the Field.

Everywhere he went the same pattern emerged; a welcome from his hosts followed by a visit to their asylum, an evaluation of the work and suggestions for its organisation or improvement, often accompanied by an offer of help in the way of grants-in-aid. Only once during the five months did he stay in a hotel: for the rest he was glad to avail himself of the close fellowship of his colleagues and friends, who represented a rich variety of national background and denominational allegiance so that, from the first, the Mission was utterly and completely international and interdenominational. On April 22nd 1887 Mr. and Mrs. Wellesley Bailey boarded the P & O steamer *Coromondel* at Bombay and sailed for home, having visited 20 leprosy asylums and other institutions already aided by the Mission, and many other centres where needs would be met in future days.

One important action which followed Mr. Bailey's tour was the reorganization of the Dublin Committee, so that its stronger representation would keep pace with the growing support at home and the increasing responsibilities overseas. The Marchioness of Dufferin and Ava, wife of the Viceroy of India, whom he had met while he was in Calcutta, became Patroness of the Mission, while His Grace the Lord Archbishop of Dublin accepted office as its President. Civic leaders in India and senior workers of co-operating Societies at home became Vice-Presidents of the Mission and their knowledge and experience were to prove invaluable.

A further result of the tour was that Mr. Bailey could now travel to the towns and cities at home where support was forthcoming, giving talks on the work which were authoritative and challenging; everywhere new friends were recruited and old friends were inspired.

CHAPTER VIII

THE HERO OF MOLOKAI

When, oh, when shall it be given to me
   To behold my God?
Oh, when shall I see my well-beloved Lord!
   Prince of the Heavens is He,
Guardian of my soul, my hope, my Saviour.

A hymn from Molokai

Wellesley Bailey's contemporary, Father Damien, died on the Isle of Molokai on April 15th 1889 after serving the leprosy sufferers of the island for sixteen years. He had contracted leprosy in 1885 and the fact that a healthy young priest with a clean hereditary background could fall prey to the disease shattered the theories of those who still argued that leprosy was the result of heredity and not contagion. His death in such circumstances focused international attention upon the disease, and the controversy between Robert Louis Stevenson and the Rev. C. M. Hyde, D.D., sharpened the interest. Dr. Hyde had written an article in *The Congregationalist* giving what he called "a careful and candid estimate" of Father Damien's work on Molokai, but in it he made charges against the priest's moral character as well as throwing doubt on the worth of his work. Robert Louis Stevenson, who had visited Molokai, rebuffed Dr. Hyde in an "open letter" which was reprinted throughout the world. Amongst those influenced by the various tributes paid to Father Damien was Frank Harris, a London editor who pleaded for the inauguration of a fund for the study of leprosy and its cure. He declared: "The only worthy memorial to him (Father Damien) would be to make his self-sacrifice final by eliminating the foul disease from the world". The Editor's plea reached H.R.H. Prince Edward, the Prince of Wales, who promised to back the campaign by becoming its Patron. With the funds raised, a team of doctors was appointed to study leprosy under Sir Jonathan Hutchinson, head of the College of Physicians. Unfortunately Sir Jonathan Hutchinson was already biased in favour of an outdated theory that leprosy was caused by the eating of stale fish—a theory already completely disproved by the Norwegians who, under Dr. G. H. Armauer Hansen, had established "the best school and hospital for leprosy in modern Europe".

One good effect of the National Leprosy Fund was the work of a Commission which it sent to make a survey of leprosy in India during 1890-91. Lord Curzon, Under Secretary for India, was Chairman of the Commission, the other members being Edward Clifford, biographer of Father Damien; Dyce Duckworth, M.D., LL.D., G. A. Heron, M.D., F.R.C.P., Jonathan Hutchinson, LL.D., F.R.S., and N. C. Macnamara, F.R.C.S. The Commissioners spent five months visiting asylums and other institutions investigating the disease and its treatment. All of the centres aided by the Mission to Lepers in India were included in the tour and the Commissioners were impressed by the work of the Mission.

It was, of course, a fact-finding investigation and population, poverty and similar conditions were assessed in depth, province by province. After examining over 2,000 cases of leprosy in the areas covered, the Commission came "to the conclusion that leprosy in India cannot be considered an hereditary disease, and they would even venture to say that the evidence which exists is hardly sufficient to establish an inherited specific predisposition to the disease by the offspring of leprous patients to any appreciable degree", a conclusion which was in line with Wellesley Bailey's own investigations. The members of the Commission were divided on the effects of contagion, although they agreed that "leprosy was an infective disease, caused by a specific bacillus, and moreover a contagious disease".

Although Dr. Hutchinson was at pains to establish his own theory of fish-eating and leprosy, the other members of the Commission came out against the theory, largely because they had met so many leprosy victims who had never eaten fish, yet still had contracted the disease.

As the investigation took place as early as 1890-91, the report of the Commissioners is striking, for it shows that Wellesley Bailey and his contemporaries were already finding encouragement along three lines of treatment—hygienic, medical, and surgical, even though the direct conclusion of the Commission was "that the incurability of leprosy by any means yet known is unfortunately certain". Palliative treatment was, nevertheless, possible with oils and other distillations as the chief agents. Some medicines, taken internally, left the patient's condition, "as bad as, or even worse than, it was before" but external application of any one of about eleven different oils left the patient better for the treatment.

Surgical "nerve stretching" in cases of painful and distressing neuralgia was hopeful but never permanent, while treatment for eye complications was in its infancy. The final conclusion was "that in any well-organized asylum no operation need be refused. Indeed the leper may be treated like any ordinary surgical patient in a general hospital".

When the Commission's findings were made known, the Government of India began to examine its own responsibility for the estimated five hundred thousand leprosy sufferers in its territory and, as is so often the case, the publication of the facts led to panic legislation which included the compulsory segregation of "beggar lepers" of which more will be said later. As has been said so forcefully, "compulsion not compassion, was to be the watchword", and the legislation failed. Meanwhile, Wellesley Bailey and his colleagues could feel that, within the limits of their resources, their part in leprosy relief was advancing in every direction after seventeen years of service. The asylums for the maintenance of which they were now responsible were seven in number; Asansol, Bhagalpur, Chandag (Pithora), Lohardaga, Mandalay, Neyyoor, and Purulia, with Bhandara and Raniganj on the drawing board, so to speak. Three other asylums received about two-thirds of their support from the Mission, and eight others were aided to a greater or lesser extent. At five institutions which did not require help for maintenance, the Mission provided for Christian instruction. Altogether, thirty centres in India, Burma, Ceylon and China, representing twelve Missionary Societies, were now assisted in their leprosy work.

Chapter IX

THE ROAD TO CHANDAG

> *I argue not
> Against Heaven's hand or will, nor bate a jot
> Of heart or hope; but still bear up and steer
> Right onward.*
>
> John Milton

A short paragraph in the Mission's Report for the year 1891 raised a tremendous sense of sympathy and compassion for a girl whose life and service was to influence Wellesley Bailey and the Mission's supporters to an astonishing degree. It read: "The Secretary's appeal on behalf of European Lepers will awaken chords of sympathy in many hearts; but most deeply pathetic is the story of how our staff of workers among the lepers, has been so strangely reinforced by the addition of a lady missionary of one of the American Societies, who has contracted the disease in the course of her work in India. The Committee have appointed her as an agent in one of our Asylums, as it is her earnest wish to spend her remaining strength in this special work to which she has been so mysteriously consecrated. We ask the prayers of our friends for her, that she may be sustained by the loving hand of God, and may be made in her days of suffering a messenger of mercy and comfort to many of her fellow sufferers".

The girl was Mary Reed and when she contracted the disease she was not in contact with leprosy patients as part of her work, being a teacher with the Methodist Episcopal

Church in America at their Cawnpore Zenana Mission, where she was appointed in 1884, just prior to her thirtieth birthday. When her health began to fail she was sent to the hill station of Pithoragarh in the Himalayas where she studied language, and assisted Miss Budden whose father was in charge of the leprosy homes at Chandag and Almora. Further service followed at the girls' boarding schools in Cawnpore and Gonda but ill-health continued, and Mary Reed returned to America in the hope that diagnosis and treatment for her illness would follow.

The nature of her illness baffled the doctors in America, as it had her friends in India, particularly a peculiar tingling in the forefinger of her right hand and an insensitive spot on one cheek. Constantly, her thoughts returned to the leprosy sufferers in Chandag and her memory of early leprosy seen there was confirmed as she read medical literature. A specialist in New York and two specialists in London confirmed her worst fears. It was leprosy!

Mary Reed did not tell her mother of the verdict until she was back in Bombay, when she wrote, with characteristic courage: "I shall have the joy of ministering to a class of people who, but for the preparation which has been mine for this special work, would have no helper at all, and while I am called apart among these needy creatures who hunger and thirst for salvation, for comfort and for cheer, He who has called and prepared me, promises that He Himself will be to me as a little sanctuary where I am to abide, and, abiding in Him, I shall have a supply of all my need. He has enabled me to say not with a sigh, but with a song, 'Thy will be done'." Though the letter came as a shattering blow to her loved ones, her mother was able to say. "The concluding words saved the day, and we felt that if Mary could sing while working among lepers, as a leper, we too should do some singing and working over here."

Sunny Crest Cottage was built at Chandag for Mary Reed and here she lived and served until her death in 1943 at the age of 88. John Jackson, Miss E. Mackerchar and Donald Miller have all told the story of Mary Reed, but it cannot be recounted too often, for her courage and faith, her devotion and service are without parallel in the history of the Mission. Three times her health improved sufficiently for her to leave Chandag but she was glad on each occasion to return "Home" to her beloved Sunny Crest Cottage, and here she welcomed visitors through the years, amongst them Wellesley Bailey, W. H. P. Anderson, John Jackson, Frank Oldrieve, Ernest Muir and Donald Miller. Her forty-two years of service to the leprosy sufferers of Chandag made her name a household name throughout the world. Her funeral at Chandag, when, "tear-stained sufferers dropped the floral offerings from their little gardens into her resting-place on the grassy slope in front of the women's chapel," mirrored the sorrow felt throughout the Mission.

Chapter X

OPEN DOORS IN THE FAR EAST

*I stopped to watch the baby chickens feed awhile;
And as they scratched for worms,
My gloom was gone,
And I
Found I could smile.*
             Hayashi—a Japanese leprosy patient

Leprosy was probably known in China long before written records were kept, but the written evidence is enough to show that the disease was feared as "the great disease" and its victims were treated as outcasts of society as much, or even more, than in India. The first China missionaries to bring the plight of leprosy sufferers to the notice of Wellesley Bailey did so in 1890 as the Report of the Mission for that year indicates:

"The Committee have received earnest and touching appeals from missionaries in China asking us to help them in dealing with the numerous lepers with whom they are brought into contact. In view of the facts laid before us, we have felt compelled to entertain their application."

The following year, at the Mission's Annual Meeting, Dr. P. B. Cousland of the English Presbyterian Mission in China was able to support a resolution, unanimously adopted: "that having heard of the urgent need of medical relief and Christian teaching for lepers in China, we approve of the action of the Committee in giving favourable consideration to the appeals that have reached them from missionaries labouring in China". The first grants made as a result of the widening field of interest were "£200 each to establish hospitals at Hangchow and Swatow, with £50 each for maintenance; the former to be under the care of Dr. Duncan Main, C.M.S., and the latter under that of Dr. Lyall of the English Presbyterian Mission; £25 per annum to assist Dr. Horder, C.M.S., in his hospital at Pakhoi, and £6 a year to the Rev. J. S. Collins, C.M.S., at Lo Ngwong, to support a Christian leper who devotes his time to teaching afflicted brethren in the leper village". It was clear that this expansion of the work was bound to continue and an appeal was made to raise the annual income of the Mission to £5,000.

Dr. Main lost no time in building the hospital for which he had pleaded with such fervour during his Scottish furlough, and on St. Andrew's Day 1892 the new building was dedicated and opened to receive its first group of male patients. The doctor's joy in seeing their comfortable quarters made him more keen to see a similar home for his female patients, and only a fortnight passed before he sent off his request for further help.

"By-and-by you must build me a small place for women ... of course you would need to increase your grant ... The last few weeks our hearts have been made sore by a poor woman leper in a putrifying condition begging us to take her in. Of course we cannot have men and women together. Pray over this, and see what you can do".

Needless to say, Dr. Main got his women's annexe and, later, a beautiful new Leprosy Home high above the lake in Hangchow.

In the interests of consistency, and with understandable pride, the 1892 Report was headed "Mission to Lepers in India and the East", a step ratified at the Annual Meeting of the Mission held on March 30th 1893 when it was resolved that: "inasmuch as The Mission to Lepers in India have now extended their operations to China and Japan, the title of the Society be for the future, "The Mission to Lepers in India and the East". Wellesley Bailey looked at the world map and prayed: "Not only here, Lord, but wherever there is need"!

Just as the support of leprosy work in China sprang from service already being carried out by missionaries doing general missionary work in that country, so the interest of Wellesley Bailey in the needs of Japan's leprosy victims began when he received a letter from an English woman, Miss H. Riddell, serving with the Church Missionary Society. She wrote, in 1893:

"Kind as the Japanese are to suffering generally it is a very usual supposition that leprosy is not a disease according to the law of nature and having no natural cure, those afflicted by it cannot therefore be of the same order of humanity as others. It would seem that for the lepers there is no hope either in this world or the next, unless we take it to them".

As usual the response was immediate, and £200 was sent so that a building might be erected to house some leprosy sufferers, with a promise of further help when required. Within two years a Leprosy Hospital was opened on a four acre site at Kumamoto, on the island of Kiushiu. Nearby was a temple of special significance to leprosy sufferers who sought a cure by ritual and rite, and Miss Riddell, some time later, contrasted the situation at the Temple with that prevailing at the Leprosy Home. At the Temple were scenes of degradation, misery, and vice, whereas at the Hospital sufferers found hope, fellowship and loving service.

Another piece of Japanese leprosy work that was helped by the Mission was that carried on by an American missionary, Miss Youngman, serving in Tokyo with the American Presbyterian Mission. In her initial letter of appeal sent to Mr. Bailey in 1893, Miss Youngman told of three Christian leprosy sufferers who had been shut away by their relatives who were ashamed of the social consequences of the disease. A group of Christians had formed themselves into a *Kozensha* or Council, pledged to help those in need, and a Japanese convert and his wife were willing to devote their lives to the sufferers if only a building could be erected for their care. The Mission's response was to send a gift to Miss Youngman, encouraging her to build the much needed shelter.

It is significant that the first patient to be admitted to the new Home was a woman who had been promised hospital treatment only on condition that she would offer her body for dissection after death but, as she lived on, the general hospital authorities were prepared to dismiss her with no place to which she could turn. Tsushima, the woman in question, was carried in a sedan chair to Miss Youngman and soon became much better. The second inmate was a carpenter who was given tools and wood so that he could erect a rough room until the permanent buildings were completed. These two were only the first in the queue and they were followed by a constant stream of needy sufferers so that Miss Youngman declared, "We can count on nobody's help but yours yet, though we are hoping for it from other quarters .... I never felt such a great responsibility as since this work has been laid upon me. But it is certainly laid upon me by Him who can never err, and so I can rest on His promise 'as thy days so shall thy strength be'."

Such were the kind of workers who turned for help to Wellesley Bailey, his Committee, and the growing army of supporters of The Mission to Lepers in India and the East.

From the simple beginnings in 1874, the Mission had already accepted part or whole responsibility for Hospitals and Homes in India, Burma, China and Japan, working with twelve different Missions or Societies, and the gross income had risen from £579 in 1875, to £5,512 in 1892.

Chapter XI

THE FIRST NATIONAL AUXILIARY

We are not storehouses, but channels,
We are not cisterns, but springs,
Passing our benefits onward,
Fitting our blessing with wings:
Letting the water flow onward
To spread o'er the desert forlorn:
Sharing our bread with our brothers,
Our comfort with those who mourn.

Anon

With the increasing responsibilities undertaken on the Field, and growing support coming from different parts of the British Isles, it was inevitable that more Christians in the lands of affluence should become interested in the compassionate service of the Mission, and offer their help. Wellesley Bailey had written many articles for the Christian press, giving an account of his journeys in India, and in 1888 he published his first book, *A Glimpse at the Indian Mission Field and Leper Asylums*, following it in 1891 with a companion volume, *The Lepers of our Indian Empire*. The first printed history of the Mission was also issued in 1891, coming from the pen of Miss H. S. Carson, of Dublin, who had supported the work since 1874. In spite of being blind from the age of twelve, Miss Carson had achieved considerable success as a writer, using her affliction as a door of opportunity into compassionate witness and service. These books brought the name of the Mission and the story of its work before a

WITH STRANGE SURPRISE

new and substantial audience who had hitherto been unreached.

In the autumn of 1892 Mr. Bailey paid his first visit to Canada and the United States of America, and in both countries spoke to groups of Christians who were moved by his first-hand reports of leprosy work. His second tour of India, undertaken in 1890-91 had shown him what could be done when simple medical care, loving attention and Christian teaching were offered to the outcast sufferers. Though he praised the work of secular institutions, he saw the difference it made when patients began to know, and accept, the love of Christ.

In churches and chapels, schools and drawing-rooms Wellesley Bailey challenged his hearers with facts which could not be contradicted, and with stories which could not be forgotten. "The work must be better known and better supported", he wrote, and his trans-Atlantic journey did much to spread the knowledge and to gain support.

So far as we know there was only one place he visited where they pleaded with him to return before leaving for home! This was Guelph, Ontario, and his contacts there were to have far-reaching results for the Mission. Mrs. James Watt and her daughter Lila, organised a meeting in their Guelph home; among those present was a young man named William Henry Penny Anderson, who was to follow Mr. Bailey in the leadership of the Mission in God's good time. Miss Watt was so impressed by Mr. Bailey's message that she determined to pass on the message to others at every available opportunity. Groups of helpers were formed in Guelph, Hamilton, Toronto and other towns, preparing the way for the formation of a Canadian Auxiliary of the Mission. In 1895 the Rev. David Herron, who had been one of the Honorary Secretaries for India, while serving at Chakrata in the North West Province of India, paid a visit to Canada and undertook a deputation tour of Canada and the United States of America. The Mission Report for that year said of him: "It is most remarkable that at a time of life when most men retire from active work and take off their armour, Mr. Herron should seem to be putting his on with renewed vigour. He has been indefatigable in his labours, travelling about in the depth of winter, making calls, addressing meetings, and forming new Auxiliaries". Besides the Auxiliaries, Mr. Herron also formed an Advisory Committee for Canada with the Bishop of Toronto as Chairman and representative Christian leaders as Committee members.

In America Mr. Herron's visit led to the founding of many supporting groups and helped to prepare the way for the later development of American Mission to Lepers (now American Leprosy Missions, Inc.)

Chapter XII

COLLEAGUES AT HOME

Hearts I have won of sister or brother
Quick on the earth or hidden in the sod,
Lo, every heart awaiteth me, another
Friend in the blameless family of God.

                    F. W. H. Myers

As The Mission to Lepers in India and the East attained its majority, Wellesley Bailey was forty-nine years of age and his heart was filled with gratitude to God for His faithfulness. Financially, the Mission was just holding its own on a budget of a little under £5,000—a target he himself had set a few years before. Miss Charlotte Pim still carried out her duties as Honorary Secretary from the home where the Mission had its birth, Alma, Monkstown, Dublin, whilst Wellesley Bailey operated from his Edinburgh home, 17, Greenhill Place. It was not until 1885 that Mr. Bailey was allowed the sum of £30 a year "towards his expenses". The following year, as we have seen, he became the Mission's first full-time Secretary, and later he was designated Secretary and Superintendent, and lastly, Superintendent.

In all his duties he had the unqualified support of his wife, both at home and on his arduous overseas journeys. On her fell the responsibility of ensuring that the children had an adequate home life, and both children and grandchildren loved her passionately. The eldest son, Thomas Grahame Bailey inherited his mother's linguistic gifts—she spoke and read French, German and Italian, as well as Punjabi—and when she was seventy and practically blind she studied Esperanto to examination standard. Thomas Grahame Bailey served as a teacher in India and later became a lecturer at the School of Oriental Studies, writing many books of Indian language studies. Mrs. Wellesley Bailey was also an accomplished musician, playing both violin and piano, and she encouraged her children to develop their musical talents. Wellesley, the second son, had a fine singing voice, while Harriette, the only daughter, played the piano.

Dermot Harvey Bailey, the youngest son, was killed on active service on May 23rd 1917, whilst serving as a lieutenant in the 1/8th Royal Scots.

Wellesley Bailey's younger brother, Thomas Andrew, shared Wellesley's interest in the work of the Mission, being appointed Honorary Secretary of the Mission for Southern Ireland, operating from the Cork Y.M.C.A., where he was organizing Secretary. While Mr. and Mrs. Wellesley Bailey were touring India and Burma from October 1895 to April 1896, his brother and sister-in-law took over a good deal of the office administration in Edinburgh, and also aided the deputation work by addressing a great number of meetings. On the return of Wellesley Bailey to his post, Mr. and Mrs. T. A. Bailey left for a visit to India with stops in America, Honolulu, New Zealand and Australia *en route*. The journey gave them the dual opportunity of seeing the leprosy work for themselves, and of getting to know supporters of the Mission in other lands. In 1898, Thomas Bailey was invited by the Mission to be its representative in India, it being felt that an official Secretary might be able to liaise with Government and regional officers in the many departments where close co-operation was vital for the well-being of leprosy sufferers, since the Leprosy Commission's visit to India. Mr. and Mrs. Thomas Bailey were able to establish Auxiliaries of the Mission in Calcutta and Bombay, and they gave personal attention to building plans, financial aid and legal matters, all of them far easier to deal with after on-the-spot value judgements.

To help Miss Pim with the growing volume of work, and to meet the needs of the increasing number of groups who wrote asking for information, Mr. A. T. Barber was appointed in 1899 as an organizing and deputation Secretary in Ireland. A similar appointment had been proved advantageous in London five years earlier, with Mr. John Jackson as Honorary Secretary for the metropolitan area. First, from a room in his own office in Aldersgate Street, the street where John Wesley's heart was made strangely warm under the influence of Luther's Commentary on the Romans—and later from Exeter Hall, in Central London, which had become a meeting place for London's evangelicals—John Jackson laid the foundations on which his successors have built in Henrietta Street, Bloomsbury Square and Portland Place.

In the Spring of 1890, The Mission to Lepers held its first London rally of supporters at the Exeter Hall. One of the results of the gathering was a succession of London Prayer Meetings where friends gathered to hear the latest information from the Field. At such a Prayer Meeting held in 1894 at the Aldersgate Y.M.C.A. and sparsely attended, Wellesley Bailey met John Jackson for the first time. The latter was drawn into the Mission fellowship, proving, in Wellesley Bailey's own words: "one of the best gifts ever given to our beloved Mission". For twenty-three years Mr. Jackson worked indefatigably for the Mission, gaining knowledge by visits to India, China, Japan, Hawaii, Canada and the U.S.A., and passing on that knowledge by the spoken and written word. He had great literary ability and the Mission gained immeasurably from his books and articles. His administrative gifts were wholly at the disposal of his colleagues, but he found time to launch a general missionary organisation, the Missionary Pence Association, afterwards called, All Nations Missionary Union. It served as a missionary information bureau and a recruiting group on behalf of the Protestant Missionary Societies—a work which still continues as All Nations Christian College.

Though a tireless worker, Mr. Jackson constantly fought against ill health, and on his way to the office on Monday, December 3rd 1917, he collapsed and died at Purley Station. In his tribute to his friend and colleague, Wellesley Bailey wrote: "He had the satisfaction of seeing the Income of the Mission increasing from £4,000 to £40,000, the work extending from forty centres of operation in five countries to eighty-seven in twelve, in which increase he himself had a large share".

It was this appreciation of the work of his colleagues which gained for Wellesley Bailey his affectionate name among them "the Chief", and throughout his life he warmed to their affection and reciprocated it.

Chapter XIII

TOURS AND CONFERENCES

Dream not that one hath drained the exhaustless sea,
Full pours the tide in widening stream for thee;
Lift for new liberties that conquering sign;
Shatter the severing walls with touch divine!

Samuel Johnson

Wellesley Bailey's growth in stature as a missionary statesman became clearer with every passing year and he was called upon, more and more, as a conference speaker and adviser, on all matters connected with missionary work amongst the world's leprosy sufferers. Mr. Bailey was a speaker at the Decennial Conference of Indian Missionaries in 1892, and when the massive World Congress of Missions was convened in Chicago in 1893, he was asked to address the assembly of delegates who warmed to his passionate pleading for more money and more workers to be set aside for leprosy work.

In October 1895 the traveller packed his bags and commenced his third extensive tour of the Indian sub-continent, travelling 23,007 miles in a little over six months; 11,303 miles in India and Burma, by train and steamer, carriage and horseback. Constantly his mind went back to earlier visits and his travel notes are full of contrasts, comparisons and carefully made criticisms or compliments. He was no "yes man", passing hither and thither with a set of pre-formed commendations.

At one centre, "a few leper huts in a mango grove", where he was appalled by the horrible conditions he saw, Wellesley Bailey sought out the European civil surgeon and asked him to join him in an inspection of the site. "He came very willingly", reported the visitor, "I pointed out some of the ghastly wounds, and asked him if nothing could be done to get them dressed. He said he would speak to the municipality and ask them to make a grant for a native dresser to visit the lepers and dress their wounds, and that in the meantime he would appoint a man at once if I could guarantee what he would have to pay extra for doing so, as he had no hospital or dispensary funds. I said I would gladly guarantee the small sum necessary, viz, five rupees a month".

At a second asylum, run by the municipality, Wellesley Bailey made a list of improvements necessary to bring the institution in line with his thinking, and was glad to hear later that the Collector and his officers conceded all the points brought to their attention. Many institutions were praised for their compassionate care and medical attendance, while others were chided for their lack of concern since it seemed to him that many of the cases which distressed him were allowed to suffer much more than they need have done. He was a great believer in environmental therapy, in a day when all too few shared his ideals. He loved to see well-kept gardens, clean court-yards, well-built huts, for he knew how easily the reverse conditions could bring sufferers to the edge of despair.

A moment of nostalgia came when he revisited Ambala and he recorded his feelings in a poignant note dated February 22nd 1896: "I stood on the very spot where, in December 1869, Dr. Morrison and I stood when I first visited the asylum; and I said to my companion 'We are now standing on the very spot where in a sense The Mission to Lepers originated, for it was on this spot that my interest was first awakened in these poor sufferers'. 'I will bring the blind by a way that they know not; I will lead them in paths that they have not known; I will make darkness light before them, and crooked things straight; these things will I do unto them, and not forsake them.' This verse led me to the Saviour in September 1866. How marvellously has it been fulfilled, if only in the matter of these poor lepers".

Standing in those familiar surroundings, Wellesley Bailey re-lived the experience in the fog-bound church at Gravesend and the later cataclysmic moment when he looked on a few leprosy beggars and found his vocation. Now, thirty years later, he knew more surely why God had called him into this "fellowship of suffering". With a full heart he yielded his life once more to the loving service of his Lord.

In 1897 the First International Leprosy Congress was held in Berlin, under the Chairmanship of Professor N. Virchow, and Wellesley Bailey took a great interest in its findings. The increasing interest in leprosy which he had seen roused in India coincided with the growth of medical knowledge stimulated by the work of Cornelius Danielssen, Gerard Hansen, Robert Koch and others in the laboratory and clinic. For some years there had been much controversy concerning the transmission and development of leprosy with a wide gulf separating the contagionists and anti-contagionists, both sides developing argument and counter-argument. At the Berlin conference the matter was decisively settled with Dr. Hansen and his followers fully vindicated. It was agreed that there *was* a causative agency behind leprosy, the *Mycobacterium leprae*, and that it was passed from person to person by some form of contagion as, *e.g.*, physical contact. Now the leprosy workers had a recognizable enemy and their chief target must be the bacillus causing the disease, though they realised that much education would be necessary before many of the nationals, who saw the results of leprosy in human life, began to treat sufferers as victims of a disease, and not as persons guilty of moral or social wrong.

All this, Wellesley Bailey had been preaching for years and he commented: "The great Leprosy Conference has come and gone, but we have learned nothing new. Still it is something to have had emphasized so emphatically by a Conference of the first Leprologists of the world the views that have been come to as the outcome of all recent investigation on the subject, *viz*:-

(1) The disease is communicated by the bacillus, but its conditions of life and methods of penetrating the human organism are unknown. Probably it obtains entrance through the mouth or the mucous membrane.

(2) It is certain that mankind alone is liable to the bacillus.

(3) Leprosy is contagious but not hereditary.

(4) The disease has hitherto resisted all efforts to cure it."

"No. 3 is the conclusion which interests us most", he added, and went on to explain how it would affect the policy of the Mission. "We are pleased to hear that the Conference follows in the steps of the Leprosy Commission which visited India some years ago, and affirms so emphatically that leprosy is not hereditary. With this idea in our minds, we have established our Homes for the untainted children of leprous parents, and we shall prosecute this department of our work with increasing hope, and trust that the public, hearing of the decision of the Conference, will rally to our aid and put it in our power to save many of the little ones. The children of leprous parents very possibly have a predisposition to the disease, and if left with lepers, living in the same huts, sleeping on the same beds, and eating out of the same vessels, they certainly run grave risk".

So much, in fact, was happening in India and elsewhere that leprosy workers were glad to avail themselves of any opportunity for consultation, and regular conferences were planned for the interchange of knowledge and experience. The Superintendents of leprosy institutions promoted by The Mission to Lepers were called together to such a conference at Wardha, in February 1902, and among the subjects discussed were the need for giving patients suitable occupation, the recruitment and training of staff, medical treatment and the degree of contagiousness in leprosy.

In December of the same year the Madras Decennial Conference of missionary workers took place. The Mission to Lepers was among the many missions represented. The work of the Mission was praised and special resolutions were passed commending its work and appealing for further help from Mission and Government sources.

As a missionary leader, living in Edinburgh, Mr. Bailey was able to take part in the planning and execution of a far more important conference, The World Missionary Conference of 1910, which was arranged "To consider Missionary Problems in relation to the Non-Christian World". At the Edinburgh Conference, 1,300 workers came together as nominees of missionary Societies, or other Church-based organisations and Wellesley Bailey was invited to serve on the Commission dealing with the relations existing between Missions and Governments which met under the Chairmanship of the Right Hon. Lord Balfour of Burleigh. Although Mr. Bailey was not mentioned in the list of authorities quoted, or the list of speakers who took part in the Commission's discussions, there is one passage in the long printed Report which clearly shows his influence. It reads: "Co-operation in philanthropic work is specially exemplified in what is now universally acknowledged as an important branch of missionary effort. *i.e.*, the relief and care of the unfortunate leper. In India the happiest understanding exists between The Mission to Lepers and the Government. There, in all the Presidencies, and in at least three Native States, the Mission receives substantial grants from the several Governments towards the erection of the necessary buildings, and also towards the support and upkeep of the institutions. In one Presidency the Government has placed all its asylums under the management of The Mission to Lepers. Here, by a give-and-take arrangement, the Mission agrees to receive lepers sent in by Government and to observe neutrality, in so far that it will not force its religious teaching on any of the inmates, or offer any earthly inducements to them to become Christians, while at the same time not abating its prerogative to preach and teach Christian doctrine. The Government freely acknowledges that it is to its advantage to have these Christian institutions where it can send its lepers, and the Mission as freely acknowledges that the co-operation and help of the Government is of great advantage to it in its efforts to relieve and help the leper".

Mr. Bailey was joined at the Missionary Conference by four other delegates from The Mission to Lepers; the Rev. A. H. Bestall, Mr. W. G. Place, Mr. T. A. Bailey and Mr. John Jackson.

Chapter XIV

"RECEIVE INTO YOUR CUSTODY"

"Unclean! Unclean!" and as the cry rang out
Men moved aside to let the leper pass,
In dread of contact. So he went his way,
Outcast from human pity, human love,
From intercourse with all his heart held dear,
From all the closest ties of human life!

Lucy R. Hardy

As we have seen, following the publication of the National Leprosy Fund's Report of the Leprosy Commission in India in 1893 and that of the First International Leprosy Conference in 1897, the Government of India were so disturbed that they began a series of panic measures, culminating in the Lepers Act of 1898 and its various amendments. Under the Act, leprosy beggars were to be treated as criminals requiring compulsory segregation from society; officers known as "Inspectors of Lepers" had the power to issue certificates declaring that individuals were, or were not, suffering from leprosy and, in the former cases, warrants of detention were issued authorizing superintendents of leprosy institutions to receive into their "custody" known leprosy beggars until they received discharge papers "by order of the Board or the District Magistrate". To many officials the advanced, crippled cases of leprosy seemed to be the greatest threat to public health and, as these were the ones usually forced on to the beggar line, they became the target for the implementation of the new legislation. The tragedy was that the burnt-out cases of leprosy which were no longer contagious were rounded up and segregated into the larger institutions, while the less blatant cases, some of them highly contagious escaped the net! In 1902 the Bengal Government requested that the Purulia Leprosy Asylum should become an institution under the Leper Act of 1898, and after giving the matter full consideration the Mission "deemed it wise to make the experiment". This was a very big step for the Mission to take for it meant building into the voluntary institution a Government segregation centre to which arrested vagrant leprosy sufferers could be sent.

The local Board set up to control and manage the Government Unit included the Rev. F. Hahn (who was appointed superintendent), the Rev. Dr. Nottrott, and Mr. Thomas A. Bailey. A further recognition of the Mission's work by Government was shown by the official maintenance grants, given for the first time in 1902, to the asylums at Dhamtari and Sholapur. From this time the Annual Reports of the Mission record both capital and maintenance grants from Government, though it was pointed out that such grants "in no way lessen the responsibilities of the Mission".

Much further afield, the eyes of leprosy workers and others involved in the general study of dermatology were turning to India to see if segregation of leprosy sufferers was the answer to the leprosy problem, and when the Fifth International Dermatological Congress was held in Berlin, in September 1904, Wellesley Bailey was asked to give a paper on Leprosy in India. This was a signal honour for a layman. Indeed, he found himself the only layman in a conference of medical specialists. The paper, which was a painstaking analysis of leprosy statistics culled from surveys and census reports covering the decade 1891-1901, was received with great interest and at its conclusion the speaker was given a standing ovation. The paper was later published by William Blackwood and Sons, of Edinburgh, and it reveals the awareness of Wellesley Bailey to India's needs and to the attempts being made by Missionary and Government workers to face the challenge of leprosy care and control.

In expressing gratitude for the recognition of the Mission's work which was so clearly shown at the Congress, the Committee of the Mission shared the hope given in Mr. Bailey's paper that leprosy was decreasing in India, though he had been careful to point out that two severe famines and a continuing plague could have accounted in large measure for the spectacular losses recorded by the census makers. The figures Mr. Bailey quoted showed one leprosy case to each 2,951 of the population in 1901, and one case to every 2,275 in 1891. The wave of optimism which the paper reflected was to be qualified as the years passed.

In his survey of leprosy in India, published in 1927, Dr. R. G. Cochrane wrote: "The census of 1921 estimated the total number of lepers at 102,000. If the census figures were multiplied by eight or even ten, a better realization of the true number of lepers would be obtained". The Government of India Report for 1942 stated that "the total number of cases in India is probably eight times the number reported in the 1931 census (150,000), or a total of perhaps 1,200,000".

Finally, Dr. Ernest Muir, in a paper written for the Mission in 1962: *The Control of Leprosy in India*, said: "It is calculated that there are some two million leprosy patients in India". It is against this background of further investigation that we can echo the sentiments with which Wellesley Bailey closed his Berlin address:

"In view of all the foregoing facts, and especially the success which has attended the little that has yet been done, one cannot but feel that if the Indian Government will take the matter seriously, and will do all in its power to encourage voluntary effort, and work in co-operation with all such effort, that therein lies the road to success and the ultimate solution of the leper problem; and that, given the above co-operation, it is not too much to look forward to a not very distant future when leprosy in India may be held well in check, and will gradually die out altogether."

Chapter XV

BEYOND THE SKY-LINE

We were dreamers, dreaming gently in the man-stifled town;
We yearned beyond the sky-line where the strange
  roads go down,
Came the Whisper, came the Vision, came the Power
  with the Need,
Till the Soul that is not man's soul was lent us to lead.

Rudyard Kipling

For eleven years Wellesley Bailey had handled the affairs of the growing Mission from Edinburgh, and when Mr. and Mrs. Thomas Bailey returned from their two-years of "incessant travelling and exacting labours", it was felt that "the Chief" should go to the Field for a fourth prolonged tour, with Mrs. Bailey accompanying him. The increasing co-operation of Government and Mission made it necessary for Mr. Bailey to spend a good deal of his time on the tour with Government officials and missionary workers, consolidating the present work and planning new enterprises. From the Autumn of 1906 until the Spring of 1908 the Baileys travelled the length and breadth of India bringing encouragement to the workers and hope to the sufferers. There were now more than sixty leprosy centres owned or aided by the Mission, with almost 6,000 patients under care, besides nearly four hundred children of leprous parents looked after in home and school. Meanwhile, the income of the Mission had grown under Mr. Bailey's leadership from £600 received in the first year to well over £21,000 in the thirty-second year. Apathy had given way to sympathy, ostracism had changed to compassion, and everywhere they went there were expressions of heartfelt approval from national and missionary colleagues for the work the Mission was doing.

Occasionally, a visit to an asylum he had known through the years was saddened by the absence of a beloved colleague, called Home after years of service, though there was also rejoicing at the knowledge that new workers had been raised up to take their places.

In 1913 Mr. and Mrs. Bailey undertook an even more arduous journey together on behalf of the Mission. The work in China, which Wellesley Bailey had followed with such prayerful interest since 1890, was causing the Committee grave concern. The revolution of 1911, by which the Kuomintang overthrew the Imperial Manchu Dynasty, was followed by an upsurge of nationalism which placed many missionaries in acute peril as they were ordered to leave their stations and reside in special European quarters. Not only were many leprosy workers forced to leave their patients but in some cases the patients themselves were massacred by the soldiery.

Since food was short for most citizens, the people resented any supplies reaching the leprosy settlements, and some officials even forbad the purchase of food for this purpose.

Though Wellesley Bailey was now 67 years of age, he willingly agreed to go to China to investigate the problems and confer with his colleagues in their hour of need. In the Mission's magazine he wrote: "I am to confer with the missionaries and the authorities, and, in conference with them, to see if something cannot be done to stop, for the future, the inhuman treatment of those unhappy sufferers in whose interests our work has been established. We are to visit Japan, Korea and other places in the Far East. The rough outline of the proposed tour is as follows: China *via*

Trans-Siberian route, remain until the end of May, then on to Australia and New Zealand for the hot season. Return to China, Japan etc; in the Autumn, and get back in this country in the Spring of next year. We most earnestly ask for your prayers; we do so not only for ourselves, but for all our Home Workers, upon whom my long absence will bring, as is inevitable, a greatly increased burden of responsibility and work".

The tour was enough to daunt the most seasoned traveller, but when one considers the reason for the journey, and the responsibility for making wise value judgements upon a whole series of differing situations, the stature of the travellers becomes immense. Yet, they were in good heart as they began their journey. Indeed, one who was present in Edinburgh during the days prior to the departure, remembered how Wellesley Bailey walked into the Booking Hall at Waverley station as though he were taking a local trip. "Where to?" asked the booking clerk brightly. "Two to Peking, *via* Siberia" answered the traveller as nonchalantly as if he were travelling to Glasgow! For all his light approach he knew that the journey would be fraught with difficulties but the trans-Siberian Railway route was the only alternative to a long sea journey. The Baileys left Britain on March 24th 1913, and arrived in Peking on April 5th, most of the journey undertaken across frozen wasteland. From Peking they journeyed to Hankow where they stayed at the Siaokan Leprosy Home run by Dr. H. Fowler. Both at Siaokan and Hangchow, they were glad to find fairly normal conditions, but further South, at Canton, they were introduced to their first grim warning of things to come.

The leprosy village with its population of 800 outcast victims was in chaos, and the Canton Government seemed set on destroying the village, if not its sick inhabitants. Mr. Bailey argued their case passionately before the local officials and made arrangements for many of the Christian patients to be transferred to the recently enlarged Home at Tungkun. The next stop on the tour was the riverside Home at Wuchow, where some of the patients lived on houseboats provided by the Mission. After the difficult situations which had to be faced in China, it was a relief to Mr. and Mrs. Bailey to proceed to Australia and New Zealand where the visitors had a warm reception from supporters of the mission.

The Australian Auxiliary grew out of the work of the Rev. R. J. Cullen, an Irish missionary of the C.M.S., who was in charge of the Home at Bhagalpur, India. Illness made it necessary for Mr. Cullen to leave India and he took a trip to Australia where, among many engagements, he addressed a Bible Class at the request of Mr. H. J. Hannah, a Melbourne Bank Manager. So impressed was Mr. Hannah that he henceforth gave all his spare time to gaining support for the work of The Mision to Lepers and in 1908 he was urged by the Headquarter's Committee in Britain, "to co-operate with them in organizing an Auxiliary for the Australian Dominion".

From Australia, Mr. and Mrs. Bailey proceeded to New Zealand and the old warrior's heart must have been stirred as he thought of all that had happened in his life since he had first passed between the two countries as a young emigrant.

From Mission records it seems that the first contributions from New Zealand were received in 1909, a sum of £14 being remitted by Mrs. F. Brown of Auckland. A visit by Mr. Douglas Green led to a number of new collecting centres so that by the time Mr. and Mrs. Bailey paid their visit in 1913 the work was well established and ready for the appointment of Mr. H. H. Abbot and the Rev. Frank Oldrieve as Honorary Secretaries for the North and South Islands respectively. The latter had been a missionary in India and he was destined to play a large part in the organizing of support for the Mission in New Zealand, in India and much later, in South Africa.

Though their programme of meetings and services was so full, Mr. Bailey was ever on the alert for news of leprosy sufferers and when he heard that two Englishmen and a Maori were segregated on the tiny island of Quaile off Port Lyttleton he insisted on visiting them.

From New Zealand, Mr. and Mrs. Bailey travelled north to Japan calling first at the Tokyo Home which the Mission's help had enabled Miss Youngman to establish in 1893. As the work in Tokyo developed, under a committee consisting of both Japanese and European members, the Home became a model of its kind and the visitors were greatly encouraged by the signs of progress. Miss Youngman's example of selfless service to the hapless leprosy sufferers influenced Government workers in the planning of their own leprosy institutions and at Osaka (and later at other Government institutions) the Mission was able to co-operate by providing facilities for Christian worship. Always ready to give credit where it was due, the visitors spoke highly of the accommodation provided for the leprosy patients at Osaka by the Government and wished that the Mission could provide similar accommodation.

The same interest in a Government leprosy service was evinced when the Baileys made a brief visit to Manila where the Mission's sole responsibility lay in the provision of an evangelist to work amongst the leprosy patients on the Island of Culion. Suspected leprosy victims in the Philippines were first sent to a Lazarette at Manila for screening and any who were found to have contracted the disease were then sent to the segregation centre on Culion. Mr. Bailey was greatly impressed by the rational approach to leprosy problems on the part of Dr. V. G. Heiser of the Philippines Bureau of Health, sharing with him the hope that his segregation policy "so wisely and humanely carried out, will eventually result in clearing the Philippines of this disease." Alas, in spite of the segregation of no fewer than 3,500 leprosy sufferers on Culion, leprosy continued to spread in the Philippines. The systematic and scientific approach of Dr. Heiser and his successors has brought innumerable benefits to leprosy workers both in the immediate area of operation and elsewhere, proving how acute was Wellesley Bailey's own assessment.

In Korea, which the seasoned travellers visited next, a similar programme of encouragement faced them.

The Pusan Home, which the Mission had helped to establish in 1910, was now superintended by the Australian Presbyterian Mission, whose workers had taken over from Missionaries of the American Presbyterian Foreign Mission Board, and Mr. Bailey was pleased to note the progress made; his report makes tender reference to the suffering of the patients and the devotion of the staff, serving under the superintendence of the Rev. Noble Mackenzie. Mrs. Bailey was greatly touched by a moving tribute, written by the women patients and presented to her on the occasion of her visit. The message began:

"Dear English Mother,

Thanks be to the grace of our God. Thanks also to those who, although they have never seen us, yet by God's grace think of and help poor lepers; and to you and the Superintendent, who have come many ten thousands of *li* to visit us, our gratitude is great beyond expression. Now that you and our Superintendent are going, we send by you to the parents and brethren in the West our salutations and grateful thanks...."

Greatly heartened by such show of appreciation of their leadership, Mr. and Mrs. Bailey passed to Kwang-ju, the second Home built in Korea with the Mission's help, and then to Taegu where, as at Kwang-ju, the co-operating agency was the American Presbyterian Mission. At Taegu the need for a new Home was laid before the visitors by Dr. Fletcher, a need emphasised by "a deputation of unhappy lepers—to the number of twenty". "It was a bitterly cold day", Mr. Bailey later reported to his colleagues at home, "and I can tell you as we looked on them shivering there and realised what this severe winter, just beginning, must mean to them, our hearts felt very sore for them".

As if to strengthen his plea for urgent consideration of the Taegu scheme, Mr. Bailey went on:

"And now, what shall I say of the urgency of this matter? I fear you and the Committee will think that I make every place out as urgent, but what can I do? The facts are as I state them, and was I not sent out with the development of the work as one of my chief objects?"

The initial cost of the Taegu project was reckoned to be about £1,000, and the visitors joined Dr. Fletcher and Mr. Macfarlane in a season of earnest prayer that God would set His seal upon their plan by laying the burden they felt upon the hearts of supporters at home. The sequel was announced in the April 1914 issue of *Without the Camp*, the Mission's magazine, where it was announced that a generous donor in Surrey had sent a cheque for £1,000 which was being earmarked by the Committee for the Taegu project, and readers were asked to join in thanksgiving for "God's gracious answer to the prayers of His servants".

As the news from China continued to be reassuring the travellers were able to cut short their visit and the alterations of schedule gave them the opportunity for calling at the Straits Settlement and the Federated Malay States. Besides visiting the Island settlement at Pulau Jerejak, near Penang, where they saw the new Chapel provided by the Mission, they stayed briefly at Tebrau, Johore, where their son Dermot was living. At Kuala Lumpur, the visitors had fellowship with

Christian Brethren Missionaries who carried out pastoral visits and conducted preaching services at the Government Asylum, which had given shelter to leprosy sufferers since 1890. At Singapore they discussed with the Bishop the possibility of similar Christian Ministry at the Government Leprosy Home. These contacts with the Anglican and Brethren workers began an association which has persisted to this day, and they are an indication of the immense value of Mr. Bailey's personal approach. Passing to India in February 1914, the travellers spent two days in conference with Missionaries of the Canadian Baptist Mission concerning the building of a new Home at Vizianagram, in the Madras Presidency, before going North to Calcutta where they booked their passage home, and paid visits to Raniganj, Naini, Rurki and Saharanpur, at each centre bringing comfort to the patients and encouragement to the workers, some of whom were now old friends of "the Chief". Once again the official itinerary made it possible for the travellers to pay a more personal visit, this time to their son, The Rev. T. Grahame Bailey, and his wife, who were missionaries serving at Wazirabad.

In a message to supporters, printed in the July, 1914, number of *Without the Camp*, Mr. Bailey included a statistical summary of the tour. "It will give you a little idea of what these journeys mean when I tell you that they represent travelling in sixteen countries; 21 steamer trips; 115 nights on steamers; 24 in trains, 123 in Mission Houses, 53 with relatives, 70 with other friends, and 18 in hotels. We visited 11 Chinese cities or towns; 7, Japanese; 4, Korean; 5, Malayan; 18, Indian; 1, Philippine; 11, Australian, and 9, New Zealand. We visited 26 Leper Asylums, and between us, gave 153 addresses". When it is remembered that the thirteen months of travel included long sessions of interview with Missionaries and Government workers, and a continuing flow of correspondence requiring attention, it would be difficult to find a better record of concentrated effort as that showed by the two travellers, both approaching seventy years of age.

They came back to their work on the "home" side of the Mission greatly encouraged by what they had seen and heard, but challenged with an overwhelming sense of unmet human need. The "Chief" closed his message: "We are needing enlargements everywhere, we are needing new buildings in many places, and are starting work in several new centres. All this means a largely increased annual expenditure and an immediate outlay for buildings. I have now been nearly forty-five years in this work, and am more convinced than ever of the great need, and of the blessing that is in store for all who will take a share in it".

Chapter XVI

THE THICK CLOUD

Through parched lips the broken sentence came,
"Lord, if Thou wilt—Thou canst!" A sudden hush
Comes over all the crowd—they breathless watch
That countenance Divine. Ah! contrast strange
Between the two! The kneeler's face they see
Is full of leprosy: the Healer's face
Full of compassion—And he stoops down
And lays His dear hand on that upturned face
. . . . And His loving tones
Come sweet and clearly down, as soft He said,
"I will, so be thou clean".

M. Colley

Just before the 1913-14 tour began, the Mission lost one of its two founders by the death on November 17th, 1912, of Miss Charlotte Elizabeth Pim, for thirty-eight years the faithful Honorary Secretary of the Mission; both Mr. and Mrs. Bailey paid tribute to the rich contribution she had made to the work. Mr. Bailey wrote: "The Mission originated in Ireland, where she was the first to be interested and she it was who suggested to the writer the idea of making an effort to awaken an interest in this country in the lepers of India. What that effort has resulted in is now a matter of history. There is one thing, however, of which there can be no doubt, and that is that the largest share in the success of those efforts was Miss Pim's. Her entire devotion and untiring energy carried all before them. No one could be in her presence for long without hearing something of the lepers. She was instant in season and out of season in the work which she loved so dearly".

Mrs. Bailey, whose association with Miss Pim went back to childhood, headed her tribute to Charlotte Elizabeth Pim: "A Reminiscence by One who Loved Her." In it she told again the story of how, on the way home from the Friends Meeting House, at Monkstown, after listening to the story of Wellesley Bailey's work among the leprosy sufferers in Northern India, the young woman had said: "Some of us are greatly interested and would like to help. We think we see our way to collecting £30 a year if that would help you". This was to prove the under-statement of the century, for Miss Pim was to see the annual income grow to more than £37,000 before laying down her task at the Master's call!

From the simple comforts given to a handful of leprosy beggars in North India, she had watched with unabated enthusiasm the doors of service opening all over India and spreading into other countries. At almost seventy stations representing the Mission's own and aided institutions, there were over 6,000 leprosy sufferers and about 700 healthy children, while Christian teaching was being conducted in the other institutions at eighteen centres.

Miss Jane Pim consented to take her late sister's place as Honorary Secretary of the Mission, so the link with the family and the home at Alma, Monkstown, was perpetuated.

The continual extension of the Mission's work led to a further change of name and, at the Society's Annual Meeting held in the Spring of 1914, it became simply, "The Mission to Lepers", a reminder that the work which had its origin in India had now passed into the Far East and, later Africa. Wellesley's brother Thomas, who had held the reins of administration during the Superintendent's world tour, now felt that he could retire and give himself more wholly to his ailing wife. Fortunately he was not lost to the Mission for, in 1915, he became Secretary for Ireland.

Like all international Missionary Societies, The Mission to Lepers was seriously affected by the first World War, which broke out within a few months of Mr. Bailey's return to the helm but, with characteristic courage, he faced the new difficulties as they arose. In July 1914 he had been able to write: "I remember that this is the fortieth year of our existence as a Mission, and that, during all these years, we have lacked nothing, so I have the more confidence in urging that we should make this year a notable one, in fact, the very best we have ever had".

The next month, on August 4th, 1914, Britain declared war on Germany and the international work of the Mission brought new and critical problems. "It is an unspeakable comfort" Wellesley Bailey wrote, as he reviewed the new situation, "to be able to fall back upon our gracious and wonder-working God at such a time as this, and to listen to His voice as it comes to us out of the thick cloud: 'Prove Me now herewith, saith the Lord of Hosts, if I will not open you the windows of heaven, and pour you out a blessing, that there shall not be room enough to receive it'. Surely now is the time to prove all our former protestations of trust, and in this time of darkness and anxiety to say: 'Although the fig tree shall not blossom, neither shall fruit be in the vines . . . . Yet I will rejoice in the Lord. I will joy in the God of my salvation . . .'." He particularly asked for prayer support for the German workers associated with the Mission saying: "Let us remember our German Brethren, for, while nationally we are opposed, in Christ we are brethren". The Committee of the Mission expressed the same view in a statement issued in October 1914: "Missionaries from Germany have been amongst the most devoted friends of the lepers, and several of our stations are superintended by missionaries of that country. For the brethren we bespeak the sympathy and prayers of our readers".

The following year German missionaries working in India were interned in detention camps by the Government of India. Among those detained were the Superintendents of the leprosy asylums at Lohardaga, Mangalore, Muzaffarpur, Purulia, Salur, Jeypore and Kodur. The Rev. P. Schulze, of Salur, spoke for all when he wrote: "We now feel strangers in this country we love and for which we are ready to die". Other Missionary Societies freed members of their own staff to carry on the work of the internees, and such help as possible was given to the unhappy casualties of the international conflict; help which was the more necessary since no money had come from Germany since the outbreak of war.

At home one of the new worries was the shortage and increasing cost of paper. The magazine pages were reduced from thirty-two to twenty-six, and it was decided not to issue a separate report to subscribers "but instead to give a synopsis of the work... in the July number of the magazine".

Mr Bailey and his colleagues were anxious to keep all administration costs down, so that the maximum amount could be used to offset rising costs abroad. Dear food and more patients were conditions facing the Superintendents of every home, and the following are typical cries from the heart addressed to the Mission. "I have never seen such high prices even in famine times"; "our Asylum is full .... famine conditions prevail"; "expenses for food have again increased on account of the greater number". Mr. Bailey hinted at the very position he dreaded; "should things go on as at present, *viz*, steadily increasing prices for food, a steadily increasing number of lepers asking to be taken in, and a steady decrease in income, there is bound to come a time when we shall have to call a halt". That time fortunately did not come and, as he surveyed the forty years of the Mission's service at the end of 1915, he was able to announce that every need had been met: "We can therefore unite in a sincere and grateful Amen to the Divine promise: 'These forty years the Lord thy God hath been with thee, thou hast lacked nothing'".

In spite of war conditions the Mission's work continued to expand, with the opening of new work at Oshima, Japan, and at Tengshien, in China. While large capital gifts were made to the Mission from time to time, the bulk of the donations were small ones and a new drive for giving in a day of enforced economy was launched with the slogan: "The Power of a Penny", with the object of obtaining food for the patients "by a multitude of pennies", since one penny would provide one meal for one patient.

The Easter Rebellion in Dublin caused the sudden cancellation of the Mission's 1916 Annual Meeting, and it was a reminder that there was a home-front to the conflict. Almost a month later the forty-first Annual Meeting took place in an atmosphere of glad thanksgiving that the Officers and Committee had been kept safe during the period of anxiety.

The burden of the years and the pressure of a war situation were taking their toll of Wellesley Bailey's strength and he became convinced "that the burden should be laid upon other and younger shoulders". At his request the Committee released him from his duties on July 1st, 1917, and with the full concurrence of all his colleagues, appointed Mr. W. H. P. Anderson, then the Mission's Secretary for India, as General Secretary for the Mission.

Mr. Bailey agreed to stay on the Committee as Honorary Superintendent of the Mission, so that his great experience would not be lost in future days. For many years Mr. Bailey had dealt with the bulk of administrative work from Edinburgh but it was decided that the new Chief Officer should work from Dublin, and new offices were opened at 20, Lincoln Place, Dublin, in June 1917. Speaking at the opening as one "who assisted at the birth of the Mission", Mr. Bailey said: "This Mission has been born and cradled in prayer; it has been brought up on prayer; it has been nourished on prayer, and prayer has been at the bottom of its success from the first moment in its life. We feel we owe all, under God, to the prayers of people who have been guided by His Holy Spirit. And I trust and believe that the work will be carried on in the same prayerful spirit in which it has always been to the very end—if there be an end". By this time Wellesley Bailey was the only member of the original Committee still alive and as he looked back on the forty-eight years he seemed to personify the Patriarch who stood on Pisgah's height, surveying the land from every point of the compass.

The sadness Mr. and Mrs. Bailey felt at relinquishing the leadership of the Mission was made more poignant by the news which arrived, just before the Dublin meeting, that their second son, Lieutenant Dermot Harvey Bailey had been killed in action on May 23rd, 1917. Letters poured in as news of Wellesley Bailey's retirement from the leadership of the Mission spread. from Missionary Societies which had received help through the years; from Directors and Superintendents of Leprosy Asylums he had visited and from individuals, patients and workers alike, who felt they were losing an old and dear friend.

The Mission had only begun to recover from the loss of Mr. Bailey's leadership when it was suddenly faced with the death of John Jackson, who had been his colleague for twenty-three years, and had made an outstanding contribution to the Mission's work by his literary ability, having written a number of books, and produced the magazine *Without the Camp* since 1906.

Chapter XVII

THE CLOSING YEARS

For life, with all it yields of joy and woe,
And hope and fear—believe the aged friends—
Is just our chance o' the prize of learning love,
What love hath been, indeed and is.

Robert Browning

Free from the responsibilities of office, Mr. and Mrs. Bailey did not lessen their concern for the leprosy sufferers of the world. Indeed, they were kept quite busy with the continuing correspondence which followed their retirement, and they lost no opportunity of sharing with Church groups and others, the story of the years. Armed with sets of lantern slides, made from photographs taken on their various trips, they were a familiar sight at Missionary meetings, and were always heard with moving appreciation.

In 1919 as the Great War came to an end, Mr. Bailey was able to review his fifty years of personal service to leprosy sufferers, and his historical sketch, packed with all its reminiscences, closed with a challenging call to his readers to help complete the task he had begun with such simple faith in 1869: "while acknowledging with humble gratitude God's marvellous dealings with the Mission in the past, we feel that we have as yet touched but the fringe of the work, and that 'Forward' must be our watchword. With such a record surely we ought to be able to adopt this. I have a vision! It is this, no other than to rid the world of leprosy —'the open sore of the world'—'The scourge of the ages'.

It seems to me that this is to be the consummation of our work, but it can be done only in God's way".

In June 1920, Wellesley Bailey was able to welcome to Edinburgh two of the men who were building on the foundations he had so patiently laid; Mr. W. H. P. Anderson, his immediate successor, and Mr. W. M. Danner, the Mission's Secretary for America. The former was at that time planning an important administrative change in the offices of the Mission, and in its general oversight. The London office of the Mission, 33, Henrietta Street, now became the office of the General Secretary and a new Governing Council was formed to take over the work of the old Dublin Committee, but bringing into its deliberations a far wider spectrum of knowledge and experience. The Forty-seventh Annual Report gave a list of new Council Members set out in a form which has continued to this day.

In spite of advancing years Mr. and Mrs. Bailey continued in good health but they found the Scottish winters trying and, on medical advice, they obtained relief by visiting South Africa where their son, Wellesley Bailey, Junior, was living in Pretoria. While in South Africa, Mr. Bailey took the opportunity of visiting the large Government Leprosy Asylum outside Pretoria, for whilst the Mission was not involved in the maintenance of the work, it had for a long time been giving grants for the Christian work undertaken by the Swiss Romande Mission at the institution.

The institution at Pretoria had another link with The Mission to Lepers in Sir George Turner, M.B., M.R.C.S., who had been Medical Superintendent of the Hospital, until he fell victim to leprosy and had to return to the United Kingdom, where he continued his research into the cause and the cure of the disease.

The Baileys returned to Scotland in the Spring of 1921 and, later that year, on the 13th October, they celebrated their Golden Wedding, having been married in Bombay Cathedral on October 13th, 1871. Once again, messages came in from all parts of the world as news of the event was given to the scattered members of The Mission to Lepers' family.

On returning from South Africa, they had taken up residence in a new home in Edinburgh which they named "Ambala" in memory of their first home together in India.

In honour of Wellesley Bailey, the 3rd Annual Worker's Conference of The Mission to Lepers was held in Edinburgh and "the Chief" presided, with his brother Thomas, Mr. W. H. P. Anderson, and Mr. Douglas Green, as the principal speakers.

Mr. Bailey's personal Jubilee of leprosy service had been remembered in 1919, but the year 1924 saw the Jubilee of the founding of the Mission celebrated with glad thanksgiving all over the world; in Church and Chapel, Asylum and Home. In preparation for the Jubilee Mr. Bailey helped to prepare a short historical sketch of the Mission's history for a book entitled *Fifty Years Work for Lepers* which the Mission issued in London, and sold in all the Auxiliaries. The Central Jubilee Meetings were held in London and began with a Communion Service in St. Paul's Church, Portman Square. The attendance at the Kingsway Hall, which had been taken for the afternoon and evening meetings was excellent. The founder was able to speak at both meetings, though admitting: "If I were to consult my own wishes I would just go and sit down somewhere, and listen to others speaking, and engage in prayer and praise for all the Lord's goodness to us during all these fifty years".

It was on this occasion, too, that he said: "The Mission to Lepers, I am accustomed to think, is 'a building not made with hands'. God has been the Builder thereof, and the

Founder thereof; and because of that fact, the Mission has gone on prospering and will prosper. To His Name alone, we would give all praise and glory today".

For Wellesley Bailey, the rejoicing was marred by a great personal sorrow; his beloved helpmate and inspiration—Alice, his wife—was not there to share the glad thanksgiving. At least, she was not there in the physical sense, having died of cancer, earlier in the year, on February 18th, 1924. In a spiritual sense, he was aware of that great cloud of witnesses, enriched by the loved face he would not see on earth; a cloud whose power of life was beyond death, whose nearness was more poignantly felt by faith's victory over the grave. Of the original Mission Committee, formed in Dublin, only Wellesley Bailey was still alive, for Jane Pim, who had taken the place of her late sister as Honorary Secretary, was not on the original Committee. Jane, in fact, died a few months after the Jubilee Meetings, and "the Chief" was called upon to write one more heart-felt tribute to an early supporter and faithful friend.

Another stalwart to lay down responsibilities at the time of the Jubilee, was his younger brother, Thomas. Thomas Andrew Bailey began and completed his service with the Mission in Ireland, though, in between, he served wherever the need called him. In 1894 he had been appointed Honorary Secretary for the South of Ireland and later became the Mission's Honorary Organising Secretary for India, and travelled the world in the Mission's interests. He eventually became its Home Secretary when the work was reorganised in 1917.

It falls to few men to see their work come to full fruition under the blessing of God, but Wellesley Bailey rose like a giant refreshed as each new Anniversary dawned. He was able to send a message of greeting to the supporters who filled the Caxton Hall, Westminster, on May 2nd, 1930, and he rejoiced to hear that it was one of the most successful and encouraging Anniversary Meetings of the decade. The emphasis was on Youth, and a great choir of Young Life Campaigners sang before and during the meeting.

Remembering his own avid search after knowledge when faced with his first groups of sufferers in India, Mr. Bailey followed with great interest the work of the new breed of leprologists who began where he left off—men like Dr. V. G. Heiser, Dr. Ernest Muir, Sir Leonard Rogers and Dr. R. G. Cochrane. These, and nineteen others gathered in Manila in January 1931, for an International Leprosy Conference at which the International Leprosy Association was formed; a move which was to strengthen the hands of all those engaged in leprosy service throughout the world.

The year 1934 saw the end of another decade of service and, once again, a volume of history was published, this time marking the Diamond Jubilee of the Mission. In a foreword, contributed by Wellesley Bailey, the veteran registered his gladness at being spared to see the celebration, even though his health would not permit him to travel down to London for the Diamond Jubilee gatherings.

"Naturally," he wrote, "I look back, and my heart goes up in thankfulness and praise to God for His wonderful dealings with the Mission through all these sixty years, He has provided for its needs, never permitting us to close a year with a deficit. He has provided the workers for the various ministries that have been carried on, the ministry of comfort and help, the ministry of teaching and healing, and of saving the children from falling victims to the disease of their parents, and the giving of an outlook and interest in life to those who had given up hope in anything".

One hundred and twelve leprosy institutions were now either owned, managed, or aided, by the Mission, and they represented about a dozen areas of the world including India, Burma, China, Formosa, Japan, Chosen (Korea), Africa and

South America. The co-operating Societies whose work and workers were helped by grants-in-aid now numbered seventeen in Great Britain and the Dominions, thirteen in America, and five in Europe. With each passing year, the income had increased with the work-load; £1,889,372 had been expended on the Field in the sixty years. In its own forty-seven Homes there were more than 9,000 leprosy sufferers, and nearly 1,000 healthy children. A further four thousand six hundred sufferers, and two hundred and thirty healthy children, were cared for in institutions receiving grants from the Mission. Methods of treatment and care had changed through the years but the Mission's foundation principles remained unchanged, and they could repeat without qualification: "We believe that the deepest need of the lepers is a spiritual one, and that it is fully met in the comfort and hope the Gospel of our Lord Jesus Christ brings to them. It is this which, to use words long since spoken, changes men's lives and their outlook on life".

Special Diamond Jubilee Meetings were held in Edinburgh and Dublin, as well as London, and in many other parts of the world; staff and patients joined in services of thanksgiving, and commemorative feasts, in honour of the Jubilee. The London audience was deeply moved when a telegram was read out to them which no one but Mr. Bailey could have sent. It read, simply, "Founder's Greetings; am with you in spirit today—in rejoicing and thanksgiving.—Bailey". In reply a telegram was despatched to Edinburgh: "Friends assembled Diamond Jubilee meeting, London, send congratulations and affectionate greetings".

A further significant Diamond Jubilee event was the broadcast of a B.B.C. Missionary talk by the Rev. E. B. Sharpe, the Superintendent of the Purulia Leprosy Home; a sign that the Mission, with others, had entered the era of mass communication.

The 61st Anniversary Meetings were the last such gatherings to receive a message from "the Chief" and, as the Rev. R. B. Douglas, Acting General Secretary, read out the message, he reminded his audience that Mr. Bailey had celebrated his 90th birthday a few days previously. Mr. W. H. P. Anderson, the General Secretary, was abroad at the time for a field tour which included a Worker's Conference in Calcutta; a conference which stressed the need for what we now call rehabilitation, "the reinstatement in life of discharged patients"; a recognition that the day was dawning when leprosy would become an incident in life, and not a life experience, a sign that a leprosy hospital was becoming a place from which a patient would return home, or at least be offered sheltered employment in field or farm. The conference was also notable for a new emphasis on child care, as children pronounced free from leprosy were moved from general asylum care; first to observation wards, and then to healthy children's Homes. Some of the children were even heard to sing with glee: "No more medicine—no more injections, no more leper home!"

These forward moves filled Wellesley Bailey with utter joy and he felt that his cup of blessing was running over. Often, especially in times of increasing weariness, he entered into the spirit of Simeon, with a sense of fulfilment the Gospel Saint could never know, "Lord, now lettest thou Thy servant depart in peace, according to Thy word; for mine eyes have seen Thy salvation which Thou has prepared in the presence of all peoples".

When it came, the end was peaceful and, even as he slept in his Edinburgh home, Wellesley Bailey was called home in his 91st year, on January 28th, 1937, ending sixty-eight years in the service of leprosy sufferers, and seventy-one years of Christian discipleship. In his closing days he faced life and death with calm assurance and unwavering faith, conscious only that both were the gift of God and were but the preliminaries to eternal joy. It had been a *good* life in every sense of that oft-abused term.

Chapter XVIII

THROUGH GATES OF SPLENDOUR

Think—
Of stepping on shore, and finding it Heaven!
Of taking hold of a hand, and finding it God's hand;
Of breathing a new air, and finding it celestial air;
Of feeling invigorated, and finding it immortality;
Of passing storm and tempest to an unbroken calm;
Of waking up, and finding it Home.

Anon

The news of Wellesley Bailey's death passed quickly round the world, and messages of thanksgiving for his life of service poured in from every quarter. At the regular meeting of the Council of The Mission to Lepers, held on March 16th, 1937, a minute was passed by the members, who included many who had served with him at home and overseas, through the years. The Minute read:

The Council of The Mission to Lepers in placing on the records of the Society the death of Mr. Wellesley C. Bailey at his home in Edinburgh on Thursday, January 28th, of this year, desire to render thanksgiving to God for the devoted life and work of His servant. The Council rejoice that it was given to Mr. Bailey to labour for so many years on behalf of the lepers and also to see the remarkable development of the Christ-like work he was led to initiate.

Mr. Bailey's sympathy for the lepers with whom he first came in contact in his early missionary service in the Punjab, India, and his desire to bring them spiritual comfort and alleviation of their physical distress, led to the founding of The Mission to Lepers in the year 1874. He became the first General Secretary of the

> Society and later Superintendent, which office he held until his retirement in the year 1917. Under Mr. Bailey's leadership the Mission's work was extended from India to China and other countries, with growing and widespread support for its objects. Thus it became international in character.
>
> Mr. Bailey's gracious personality, his humble-mindedness, his strong but simple faith, his capacity for securing the co-operation of others in different parts of the world who became fellow-workers with him, and his readiness to give credit to all for the results obtained, caused him to be held in enduring respect and affection.
>
> The Council believe the work of The Mission to Lepers so commenced and continued must constitute a Memorial to Mr. Bailey whose name is inseparably associated with it.

From among the many tributes which were offered from all parts of the world, the following quotations give an indication of the love and regard in which "the Chief" was held by his fellow-workers.

"In him, as he considered the condition of these poor sufferers, was something of the very spirit which was in the heart of our Saviour when, moved with compassion, He put forth His hand and touched the leper. And like that of our Lord, his pity was no mere emotion; it evoked constant service, lovingly given. All who are interested in the work of the mission should pray that Mr. Bailey's example and influence may abide with all who are called to carry on this work, and stimulate them to fresh endeavour". (The Most Rev. C. F. D'Arcy, D.D., Archbishop of Armagh, President of the Mission).

"We give thanks to God for the work Mr. Bailey was permitted to do on behalf of the lepers in India and other countries and for sparing him for so many years to see its remarkable development. The work he did so notably and the memory of his kindly life will continue to be a stimulus and an example". (Sir William Fry, D.L., Chairman of the Mission Council).

"Some have accomplished great things but the beauty of their service has been marred by the assertion of self, but not so with Wellesley Bailey. We call him the 'Founder' of the Mission, but he said: 'there was not any human founder ... God was at the back of it'." (Mr. A. T. Barber, Hon. Secretary of the Mission).

"The Nineteenth Century was a period of remarkable developments in the spreading of the Gospel throughout the world. William Carey was laying the foundations in India, Livingstone went to Africa, and Hudson Taylor to China. But the Lord's messengers are many and their ministries are manifold. In the person of ... Wellesley Bailey a work for the help of those suffering from Leprosy in India was commenced in 1874 which has spread abroad ... Mr. Bailey was spared for sixty-three years to see the wonderful results springing up from a small beginning". (Mr. Walter B. Sloan, F.R.G.S., Acting Chairman of the Council).

"The memory of Mr. Bailey will abide in the hearts of all who knew him, especially those who at one time or another were associated with him in service and, not least, his memory will endure in the Homes of the Mission where his name is venerated". (Mr. W. H. P. Anderson, General Secretary of the Mission).

"Keenly interested as he was in every detail of the work so dear to his heart and wonderfully alert in mind and wise in counsel as he proved himself to be, even in these closing months, the characteristics which stand out most clearly, as I think of him, are his wonderful graciousness, his unfailing kindliness and his great humility". (The Rev. J. M. B. Duncan, B.D., Chairman of the Committee for Scotland).

"Wellesley C. Bailey was a Christian pioneer who deserves to be enrolled among the saints. His loving sympathy for the suffering lepers .... his keen intelligence in devising a way of saving them, his inspiring enthusiasm in enlisting thousands of helpers, touching their sympathetic hearts, opened an unfailing flow of money as well as of devoted service from friends he made at home, in the Dominions and in America". (Dr. Wm. Jay Schieffelin, President of the American Mission to Lepers).

"Mr. Bailey was a man of vision, wise judgement, gifted with the qualities of leadership and consecrated to the Lord Whom he loved". (The Rev. H. N. Konkle, Secretary for Canada).

"Today, because Wellesley Bailey allowed himself to be God's chosen instrument and did not resist the call, but in prayer and faith and love went forward, untold misery has been ministered unto; unnumbered lives have been saved—in the fullest sense of that word; and incalculable influence has been brought to bear upon the thought and action of men and Governments towards those who before were just avoided and feared and driven 'without the camp'." (Mr. A. Donald Miller, at a Memorial Service in Purulia, India).

Besides messages from all the overseas Committees of the Mission, Minutes of condolence and thanksgiving were passed at the Councils and Committees of co-operating Societies, including the two with which Wellesley Bailey had served, namely, The Foreign Mission Committee of the Church of Scotland and the Committee of the Zenana Bible and Medical Mission.

Two sons and one daughter survived him, together with a number of grandchildren. The Rev. T. Grahame Bailey, D.Litt., one of the sons, was on the staff of the London School of Oriental Languages, whilst the other son, Wellesley Bailey, Junior, was in South Africa. The daughter, Mrs. (Dr.) H. F. Lechmere Taylor, served with her husband as a missionary in Pakistan. Some of the grandchildren stayed with the grandparents in the Edinburgh home for long periods, whilst their parents were overseas in India and Pakistan. One of them recalls the closing years of Wellesley Bailey's life, when increasing weakness made even little tasks like the holding of a newspaper, an effort. An ex-service man was employed to take the old man out for walks, and attend to his needs, as he wished to be active until the very end. "My grandfather was not a saint", she wrote, "nor even a clever man. His great gift was that of loving kindness, and a simplicity that perhaps could not see the difficulties a more sophisticated mind might see. I do not remember ever hearing from him an ungenerous remark, or seeing him angry, except for the minor irritabilities that are bound to occur in family life". It was the simplicity of faith and life which made Wellesley Bailey the man he was, and it was the same childlikeness which enabled him to accomplish his mission on earth an ingenuous and uncomplicated faith, gained initially and strengthened constantly from his sweetheart, wife and partner, Alice Grahame. "Theirs was such a union", one of the grandchildren wrote, "that it is difficult to think of them apart", and it was a sentiment with which "the Chief" would have heartily agreed. This is the fact, more than any other, which has come to the biographer, in following the path of the years. The story that has emerged is that of two people so at one in mind and heart that they became the complement of each other's needs, and the fulfilment of each other's desire. God was indeed "at the back of it", but Wellesley and Alice Bailey were at the centre of it, and from their compassion for leprosy sufferers concentric circles of loving service spread out until they took in the world.

In the present world headquarters of The Leprosy Mission, (the name was changed from The Mission to Lepers in 1966), the Bible which Wellesley Bailey used from 1897 until his death, is kept with understandable pride. Comments, notes and quotations abound in the wide margins and blank endpapers of the Bible but most significant of all is a short comment under Isaiah 42.16: "And I will bring the blind by a way that they knew not; I will lead them in paths that they have not known; I will make darkness light before them, and crooked things straight. These things will I do unto them, and not forsake them". By the text, Wellesley Bailey had written, simply, "Gravesend, Sep.2.66. My Conversion text!" This expression of simple faith was the key to his life and work. He walked humbly with God, expecting the light to point the way forward, step by step, like the pillar of cloud and fire which led Israel through the wilderness to the Land of Promise. Writing an article for the Mission in 1919, Mr. Bailey had quoted some lines from Robert Browning, his favourite poet, and they reflect his faith admirably:

'Wilt thou adventure for My sake, and man's,
  Apart from all reward?' And last it breathed—
'Be happy, my good soldier: I am by thee,
Be sure, even to the end!'—I answered not,
Knowing Him. As he spoke, I was endued
With comprehension and a steadfast will;
And when He ceased, my brow was sealed His own.

THE LEPROSY MISSION

AUSTRALIA, W. R. Edgar, 174 Collins Street, Melbourne, Vic. 3000; **CANADA**, Rev. H. D. Graham, M.A., Suite 1128, 67 Yonge Street, Toronto M5E 1J8; **ENGLAND AND WALES**, Rev. R. J. Findlay, B.A., Dip.Th., 50 Portland Place, London W1N 3DG; **HONG KONG**, Rev. S. S. Leung, P.O. Box 380, Hong Kong; **INDIA**, Dr. Victor P. Das, 5 Amrita Sher Gill Marg, New Delhi 110003; **IRELAND (NORTHERN AREA)**, R. B. McCandless, 44 Ulsterville Avenue, Belfast BT9 7AQ; **IRELAND (SOUTHERN AREA)**, Rev. R. P. B. Mathews, 20 Lincoln Place, Dublin 2; **NEW ZEALAND**, Rev. R. A. Alcorn, 43-45 Mount Eden Road, Auckland 3; **SCOTLAND**, Rev. W. Hough, 26 Bothwell Street, Glasgow G2 6NU; **SOUTHERN AFRICA**, Rev. W. O. Maasch, 30 Seventh Avenue, Highlands North, Johannesburg; **EUROPE**, Rev. S. Perotti, 6 Rue des Fossés, 1110 Morges (Vaud), Switzerland; **NORTHERN EUROPE**, Rev. Henry Aalto, Hakolahdentie 10 A9, SF-00200 Helsinki 20, Finland; **BELGIUM**, Rev. René Clerbois, Rue Théophile Massart 13, 6518 La Hestre; **DENMARK**, Mrs. L. Stoklund, Lundevej 19, 2970 Horsholm; **FRANCE**, M. le Comte A. de Clermont, 37 rue Davioud, 75016 Paris; **GERMANY**, Freiherr A. von Rothkirch und Panthen, 821 Prien am Chiemsee, Am Berg 8; **ITALY**, Rev. Guido Mathieu, Via Pasteur 60, 18012 Bordighera (IM); **NETHERLANDS**, Rev. C. Eijer, Hommerterweg 222, Amstenrade; **SPAIN**, Pastor Humberto Capo, Calle Bravo Murillo 85, Madrid 3; **SWEDEN**, Rev. Jean Malm, Nygatan 58, S 702 11 Orebro; **SWITZERLAND**, Pfarrer E. Hunzinger, 4622 Egerkingen, Postfach 22.